SARTRE AND DRAMA

by Robert Champigny

In Memoriam Lord Chafou

CONTENTS

INTRODUCTION

Dramas are meant to be performed rather than simply read. Reading dramatic fiction does not fully differentiate it from narrative fiction. On the other hand, performances of a dramatic script vary. A particular drama is thus indefinitely multiplied.

My analysis is not about various performances of Sartre's scripts. It is about the texts themselves as I have read and reread them. Still, I consider them as scripts to be performed as well as read. Certain differences between dramatic and narrative fiction can thus be emphasized.

I shall examine the dramatic texts in relation to other writings of Sartre, in particular texts which comment on dramatic fiction in general and on particular plays. What must be rejected in considerations of this sort is of course the postulate that a writer's practice is automatically an excellent illustration of his theories. Valéry, for instance, wrote much, and well, about pure poetry. But his poems contain strong dramatic and narrative, i.e. prosaic, elements. By itself, this remark is not an unfavorable judgment. One may prefer applied poetry to pure poetry, or enjoy them equally.

The first part of my analysis extracts some theoretical points from various essays of Sartre, and develops a critical discussion. The second part deals with the dramatic scripts. It does not attempt a comprehensive exposition of each text. It concentrates on several points which I thought interesting, mostly within the perspectives indicated in the part on theory. The conclusion of my analysis contains a comparison between Sartre's plays and some others, also published in the nineteen fifties, which contribute to making this short period one of the most brilliant in the history of French drama in my judgment.

PART I

THEORY

In *Un Théâtre de Situations (A Theatre of Situations),* Michel Contat and Michel Rybalka have collected short texts in which Sartre talks about dramatic art. In interviews, which are also included in this volume, Sartre explains and defends his own plays, more seldom criticizes them. Particularly interesting are the pieces entitled *Théâtre épique et Théâtre dramatique, Mythe et Réalité du Théâtre,* and the interview conducted by Paolo Caruso on the subject of one of the plays, *Les Mains Sales (Dirty Hands).*

The paragraphs which follow discuss questions that are raised in *A Theatre of Situations.* But I also refer to other writings of Sartre, especially *L'Etre et le Néant (Being and Nothingness)* and *Qu'est-ce que la Littérature? (What is Literature?*). Page numbers in this first part refer to *Un Théâtre de Situations,* unless otherwise indicated.

DRAMATIC BEHAVIORISM

A dramatic character may talk about his feelings, beliefs, desires. But, unless the clumsy device of an authoritative offstage voice is used, a drama cannot furnish narrative axioms about psychological happenings and states of affairs. A novel, on the contrary, can tell us what a character is feeling and thinking with the same certainty as descriptions of external events. A novel can resort to interior monologues; a drama has to externalize them.

Sartre alludes to this difference when he says that dramatic art is not "psychological." It had better be said that its approach to psychology has to be behavioristic. The audience is presented with stimuli and reactions. The inside of a character is a black box. The audience has to make psychological inferences from the overt reactions considered as symptoms. These inferences may differ from what a character says about himself or others. An angry reaction may be interpreted as a symptom of fear. If a character says he is afraid, this statement, by itself, may simply show that, for some reason or other, he chooses to assume the part of someone who is afraid.

In this respect, dramatic art remains closer to ordinary conditions than do novels which exploit the possibility of describing the inside of a character axiomatically. Ordinarily, unless possessed of special powers, we have to observe the overt behavior of others to infer, rightly or wrongly, what they feel, believe, desire, think, intend. To some extent, we have to do this even as regards ourselves. Introspecting is like Orpheus turning round to see Eurydice, rather than like Narcissus looking at his image. Orpheus has to substitute words for Eurydice.

HUMANISM AND TOTALITARIANISM

Dramatic logic is the dialectic of stimuli and reactions between characters, also between a character and himself, since he reacts to his own reactions. This dialectic takes place mostly between anthropomorphic characters. In his theorizing, Sartre goes further. He proceeds as if dramatic dialectic could take place only between anthropomorphic characters. There is some validity in the view that dramas cannot give as much importance to nonhuman elements as novels or films. Yet we have only to think of Symbolist or Surrealist tendencies to deny that dramatic dialectic is purely an anthropomorphic business. Actually, Sartre himself, in some of his plays, gives nonhuman elements a potent role, instead of reducing them to an indifferent background.

The reduction of dramatic dialectic to anthropomorphic characters in Sartre's theorizing is in accord with the simple opposition between men and things to be found in his ontological essay *Being and Nothingness* (1943). Things, or objects, are said to be in themselves, or simply to be. "Human reality" alone is said to "exist," to be "for itself" and "for others." And these others are human too. *Being and Nothingness* does not present humans as an animal species. Indeed, it leaves no room for animals.

Reminiscent of Descartes, this human chauvinism is a predominant trait in Sartre's essays in the nineteen forties and afterwards. This is not the case in the philosophical novel *La Nausée* (*Nausea*), published in 1938. In this text, the term "existence" is indistinctly applied to human and nonhuman beings. The term "being" appears in opposition, but it is applied to ideal, abstract, imaginary entities: mathematical, conceptual, fictional, esthetic. On the contrary, *Being and Nothingness* offers no special niche for such entities. And it is also to be noted that, in the essay *L'Imaginaire* (*The Imaginary*), published in 1940, no distinction is made between the imagined and the imaginary. What is interpreted as imaginary (fictional) may be imagined, but, in some cases, it may also be seen. Thus, an esthetic tree in a picture.

To my mind, the failure to make this distinction, which has many echoes in Sartre's philosophizing, is a basic flaw. It can be related to a totalitarian tendency, which Sartre acknowledges in *What is Literature?* (*Situations*, II, 320). He names Hegel as the source. Instead of stressing a radical diversity, and even disparateness, between experiences, types of experiences, types of entities (this would be my own tendency), Sartre attempts to present (human) existence, if not as a constituted whole, at least as a perpetually renewed desire and project of unification, of self-totalization. Among other things, he tends to play down the divergence between imagining fictional beings and imagining historical beings.

It is also to be noted that, in *Nausea,* a passage makes fun of various kinds of humanism, whereas the essay *L'Existentialisme est un Humanisme* (*Existentialism is a Humanism*), published in 1946, advocates a certain kind of humanism based on the simple, too simple, distinction between men and things.

GESTURES

In *A Theatre of Situations* (for instance, p. 118), also elsewhere, Sartre distinguishes between gestures and action, and stresses the former to characterize dramatic art. It is obvious that he makes the notion of gesture cover verbal as well as nonverbal manifestations. I adopt this terminological move. Using some passages in Sartre's essays as springboards, I should like to deploy the notion in a way which goes beyond what Sartre says.

"Gestural" may be used to name a mode of signification and interpretation, with an historical (utilitarian) version and a fictional (ludic and esthetic) version, the latter being particularly in evidence in plays and performances of plays, though not limited to them. The gestural mode is for me only one mode of meaning (with two main versions). Such modes as the narrative (also with two main versions), the poetic, the conceptual, the proverbial, would be equally fundamental. Sartre, on the contrary, often appears to consider the gestural mode as more fundamental than others. This is in particular the impression which I received from the passages about language in *Being and Nothingness*. His sensibility appears to be oriented mostly toward dramatic meanings and values, though he is far from blind to poetic meaning (which he labels *sens* as opposed to *signification*).

An angry outburst may be interpreted as a symptom of fear. But this is not the way (a narrative way) in which the gesturer intends his angry utterances to be interpreted. He intends his reaction to have certain effects on someone, perhaps only himself. He intends it to act as stimulus.

The gestural mode of meaning and interpretation allows personifications. What emits a signal interpreted as gesture is thereby personified to some extent, perhaps fleetingly. Intentions are ascribed to the source of a gesture. A speaking clock which says it is now four-thirty does not have to be personified at all. Its utterance may simply be interpreted as a narrative statement. It does not have to be received as a gesture designed to influence someone.

I prefer to speak of personification rather than of (ready-made) persons, in order to allow for shifts of interpretation and degrees of personification. Most often, in daily occurrences, we personify anthropomorphic apparitions, but not always (someone lost in a crowd). I personify such apparitions (and myself) to various degrees. I personify a cat more than a fly. I may fleetingly personify a hammer, consider it as a nasty traitor, if I insult it after it has hit my thumb instead of a nail. If someone prays for rain, he personifies the nonhuman entity that he addresses.

An action, in the physico-chemical sense, involves no gesture. Chemical agents are not personified. Let us call "functioning" an action without gesture, "activity" an action with gesture or reduced to gesture. In so far as something appears to be functioning like a machine, it may be called an agent; in so far as we have the impression of an activity, the agent is also an actor, in a broader sense than participating in the performance of a play.

Gesturing can be separated from functioning in various ways. If an activity with a utilitarian goal has failed, we may say that it was a beautiful gesture, thus substituting an esthetic value for the lack of utilitarian value. Or, less charitably, we may say it was a mere gesture. In *Being and Nothingness,* Sartre gives the example of a waiter who overdoes his utilitarian gesturing and thus develops a ludic (playful) gesturing. To this extent, he does not assume the utilitarian role of a waiter, moved only by the intention of functioning as a serving machine. He plays the part of a waiter as if he were on stage in front of an appreciative audience. Or he may take only himself as a spectator. He attempts to enjoy the gesturing for its own sake, so as to forget the drudgery of the utilitarian role.

A liar may be said to try to foster the illusion that his utterances are not play-acting. On the contrary, a theatrical performance allows a spectator clearly to distinguish between the utilitarian activity and the ludic activity of a comedian. A utilitarian activity takes place in the historical field; its goal is projected in the same field beyond the span of its exercise. A ludic activity takes place in a playing field detached from the historical field which serves as frame and background (the lines of a tennis court, for instance). A professional killer functions as killing machine in the historical field. An actor who plays Othello does not even pretend to kill an actress. In his ludic role, he is pure gesture. The Latin *illudere* may mean "play." But the English, or French, "illusion" is not equivalent to "lusion." So, "illusion" had better be avoided if one speaks about what is clearly interpreted as fiction.

Sartre says that there could be no dramatic art if men were "real objects" for men (p. 118). More precisely, there could be no dramatic art if they were only historical and utilitarian entities. But elements of experience which are not anthropomorphic may also be viewed as fictional, in a ludic and esthetic perspective. An astronomer considers stars in an historical perspective; but not someone who contemplates them for pleasure. A starry sky is thus an esthetic object, whether it is in a painting or not. The esthetic meaning of a starry sky tends to be more poetic than dramatic. Yet a star may be personified. To the extent that they are integrated in a dramatic dialectic, props develop some gestural meaning.

In his ludic role, an actor is *an* Othello. He is not Othello. Othello belongs to the esthetic world called *Othello*. Thus, if a play is performed, at least three perspectives of interpretation can be distinguished: utilitarian, ludic, esthetic. The three would be confused if one said: "In theatre A, actor B killed his wife every night last week at about 10 p.m."

Sartre says: "The actor is at such a distance that I can see him, but could never touch him nor act upon him" (p. 28). This remark does not apply to the actor as an historical and utilitarian individual, but to the actor in his ludic activity. An historical actor is twenty yards away from an historical spectator; he can be touched, he can be operated upon by an historical surgeon. The actor as ludic role is in a ludic field; and the character is in an esthetic field.

An Othello can be seen and heard. Othello can only be imagined like a character in narrative fiction. There have been many ludic Othellos; there is only one esthetic Othello, unless we count as different Othellos those that literary critics have composed. Criticism is a ludic activity.

In *Racine et Shakespeare,* Stendhal tells the story of a spectator who made use of a loaded revolver to prevent a blackamoor from killing his white wife. Such a spectator would have confused utilitarian actor, ludic role, esthetic character. This kind of confusion must be ruled out if one speaks of dramatic art. If, in the Aristotelian tradition, we speak of terror and pity, we should distinguish between utilitarian emotions, which are in clutch with historical events, even if one feels helpless, and played emotions. If the affective motor is kept out of clutch, terror, pity, suspense, may be enjoyed for their own sake.

An art has to limit the variety of signs to which it resorts, in order to detach ludic and esthetic existence from historical existence. A performance of a play exploits sensory signs. An Othello cannot be touched or smelled, but he can at least be seen and heard. It may be alleged that, because of this, the performance of a play is more favorable to illusion than reading a play or novel. On the other hand, people may easily turn into a ludic spectacle what they see and hear in news programs on television, or even a car accident occurring before their own eyes. This is one of the reasons why I use the terms "historical" and "utilitarian," instead of the hopelessly polysemous "real." There is a lot of fictionalization in so-called real life.

The duality between an Othello and Othello disappears if a spectator has not watched another performance already, has not read the script, or if the play-acting is improvised. It also disappears in my essay, since I do not consider performances with various actors and directors.

An object, or world, is esthetic if it is contemplated. In order to adopt this perspective toward a play, a novel, a poem, one must be acquainted with its entirety, with the end as well as the beginning. This is not the case when a text is read for the first time. The perspective is then that of a ludic activity. A ludic activity makes the uncertainty of the future pleasant. Though Sartre's plays no longer hold any suspense for me, I shall have to take the perspective of reading a play or attending a performance for the first time into consideration.

A distinction between utilitarian and ludic activities can also be made regarding an author. Lawyers are concerned with authors in the utilitarian and historical sense. A few months ago, I heard that the historical Sartre, whom I had met and whose hand I had touched, had died. In most passages in my essay, though not all, it is a ludic Sartre that is talked about. I compose him as a ludic partner and opponent for the purposes of my critical activity. I do not view him as a utilitarian ally or enemy. This ludic Sartre is a personification of a set of esthetic texts considered as roles. No doubt, relations may be established between the historical Sartre, to whom I may also allude, and my ludic Sartre. But these relations are not identities. And they are not simply similarities or contrasts. To the extent that I refer to the historical Sartre, the pronoun "I" correlatively designates an historical individual.

WORDS AS GESTURES

Utterances have a gestural meaning to the extent that they are interpreted as intended to influence the behavior of the recipient. The speaker may be the only recipient (monologues).

The basic logic of narrative or dramatic fiction is spatial and temporal. Among ludic and esthetic types of verbal meanings, this feature distinguishes fiction from philosophy and pure poetry. But, while descriptions of places, events, objects, processes, are verbal in narrative fiction, the narrative and descriptive task can be assumed by the nonverbal elements of staging in the case of the theatre. In a dramatic script, there are some stage directions; but they do not have to be judged esthetically.

The gestural aspect of meaning is particularly evident in vocatives, imperatives, interjections. The importance of intonation is such that we may roughly understand the gestural import of a dialogue in a tongue that we have not learned (a quarrel, for instance), while the narrative content remains blank.

These remarks are in accord with what Sartre says about words in dramas: "Language is a moment of action, as in life . . . Its sole purpose is to give orders, advocate, express feelings in the form of pleading (hence with an active goal), in order to convince, uphold, accuse, manifest decisions, for verbal duels, refusals, confessions, etc., in brief, always in act" (p. 134).

Taking *Antigone* as a paradigm (it seems to me *Oedipus Rex* would offer another orientation), he views the characters of Greek tragedies as litigants (p. 158). He considers that dramatic dialectic in general is a composition of conflicts, and that modern dramas add conflicts within characters to conflicts between characters: "Contradiction, now, may belong to the individual character" (p. 139).

Sharp conflicts between and within characters may be viewed as a condition of a tight dramatic dialectic. And this is nearly always the case in Sartre's plays, which often stress conflicts within characters. But, instead of that, a play can stress conflicts, or farcical incongruities, between words, without the characters appearing to be deeply involved in the process. This is the case in most of the plays I shall mention in the conclusion.

In *What is Literature?*, Sartre makes a distinction between a theatre of *caractères* and a theatre of situations. The former would consist of having characters (*personnages*) react to one another on the basis of set personalities (*caractères*). On the other hand, in a theatre of situations, "the heroes are freedoms caught in a trap, like all of us. What are the ways out? Each character will be nothing else than the choice of a way out" (*Situations*, II, 313). The same distinction occurs in *Forgers of Myths*, included in *A Theatre of Situations:* "What is universal . . . is not a nature, but the situations in which man finds himself, that is to say, not the sum of his psychological traits, but the limits which confront him on every side" (p. 57).

These declarations in favor of a theatre of situations echo the way "human reality" is analyzed in *Being and Nothingness*. In this major essay, Sartre prefers the phrase, "human condition" to "human nature," so as to stress the opposition between humans and "things." The human condition would be primarily the experience of a situated freedom, that is to say, the experience of deciding and having to decide. It is not always pleasant to have to decide. *Being and Nothingness* links the experience of freedom with the anxious feeling of responsibility. We are "condemned to be free," that is to say, to make decisions.

Freedom and situation are the two sides of one coin. Psychological traits, past experience, as well as external factors, are part of a situation. We are passively situated, but we also have to situate ourselves, to decide what the situation is. In deciding what it is, we already decide what can be done. We may decide to stay put. In the language of *Being and Nothingness,* a temperament becomes an "original choice"; a *caractère* becomes a pledge to remain constant.

To some extent, this voluntaristic conception fits the conditions of dramatic art in general. In order to posit a set personality as an axiom, a dramatist would have to make one or several characters paint a portrait of the frozen character at the start, equip him with a ready-made personality (a device which is undramatic in itself). And then the behavior of the character would confirm the portrait throughout the play. Some plays by Molière would furnish good examples. But, even if there is no prefabricated portrait, will not the sequence of reactions gradually establish a *caractère* in the form of habits? If the character appears to be changing, this mutability itself might be considered as a characteristic trait.

The important thing, from Sartre's standpoint, is to make it clear that the characters have to make decisions. According to *Being and Nothingness,* we experience our existence constantly as decisions being made. The decisions may be only choices of mental attitudes (even while asleep?). On the other hand, dramas would have to concentrate on moments in which the decision appears radical to the characters involved. Thus Sartre speaks of "the free decision which involves a morals and a whole life" (p. 20). This means arranging tight situations in which the characters are confronted with the horizon of existence (*situation limite*). In such extreme situations, "death is one of the terms" (p. 20). Death appears to the character (also to the audience?) as one of the two branches of an alternative.

This way of interpreting the phrase "theatre of situations" shows Sartre's taste for *drame* in a restrictive sense, with epic and tragic tendencies. Another way of avoiding a theatre of *caractères* would consist of downgrading the status of characters. In particular, they would not be presented as making decisions and having to make decisions. The situations and the dialectic would be loosened correlatively.

HISTORICAL AND FICTIONAL

What has been said in the preceding section about the dramatic aspect of
words and about situations may apply either to the historical and utilitarian
domain or to the fictional and esthetic domain of a play. An actor who plays
Othello kills neither an actress nor Desdemona. But Othello kills Desdemona.
Within an esthetic world, within fictionalizing brackets as it were, there may be
a duality between utilitarian (cognitive, moral) activities and ludic activities.
In *Hamlet,* for instance, the performance of a play is embedded within the play
to be performed.

Each in its own way, various arts have to extract well-assorted materials
from the messy and superabundant mixtures offered and imposed by daily life,
and refine them in order to isolate and compose them. Music extracts notes
from noise; pure arithmetic detaches numbers from countable objects. Dramas
select gestures in the jungle of signals, transplant them, cultivate them
in their greenhouses or walled gardens. "Extracting," "detaching,"
"refining," "isolating," "transplanting," appear to me terms better oriented
than "imitating" or "representing."

Sartre suggests that gestures most refractory to esthetic transplantation
and acclimatization are those which are tied to work: "What would the theatre
talk about, if not work? For, after all, work and action are the same thing. This
is the real intimate contradiction of the theatre" (p. 133). It is a contradiction
because Sartre does not see how work can be transfigured esthetically without
the impression of an imposture.

He appears to rely on the usual distinction between work and play,
utilitarian and ludic activity, a distinction which does not imply that every kind
of play is easier than every kind of work. Work is the same thing as action, if, by
"action," we mean a utilitarian alliance of gesture and function in the historical
field. But, by "work," Sartre also appears to mean something more precise: a
utilitarian activity which involves something else than just words or equivalent
nonverbal gestures, an activity which stresses physical contact, use of material
tools, technical knowledge and ability.

In the case of utilitarian activities with words or equivalent nonverbal
gestures, the efficacy is magical. Brains remain black boxes to a great extent.
We cannot trace (narratively) the trajectory of signals, their metamorphoses
within the brains, including our own. This is how I would interpret a passage of

Being and Nothingness in which Sartre says that humans are first of all sorcerers for each other. "And for themselves" might be added. No doubt, a utilitarian process has to go beyond such gestures at some point. But, in a drama, what goes beyond may be kept beyond (in the wings). Or it may be acclimatized to some extent. For instance, suppose that an order to kill triggers killing with a revolver. There is something magical about this procedure, since our eyes cannot follow the trajectory of a bullet any more than that of words. Killing with a sword, or a pillow, appears less appropriate in a performed drama, because the suggestions of contact, penetration, suffocation, may be too strong. The ludic and esthetic transplant may then more easily be rejected by spectators as an imposture. Or some spectators may be incited to confuse the three perspectives I spoke of: actors as historical individuals, actors as ludic roles, esthetic characters.

Sartre contends that a cardboard locomotive would be a ludicrous (rather than ludic) prop. I agree, if the context were such that it tried to evoke the locomotive as a tool, as a utilitarian machine. But the context might be such that it would let us see the locomotive with the eyes of a child playing with it or gazing at it in a toyshop window.

Another aspect of experience, the most important unfortunately, which appears to me refractory to an esthetic transplantation is grave physical pain, or rather its symptoms. One of Sartre's plays will offer the opportunity to discuss this question. Let me simply say at this point that the autonomy of a ludic role (the actor who can be seen and heard, but not touched) and of the esthetic world (imagined and imaginary) is threatened if a dramatist injects elements that tend to make ludic roles and esthetic characters lose their magical, ghostly status and the peculiar appeal that goes with it.

The ludic and esthetic autonomy of dramatic fiction may also be threatened by confusions between historical and fictional places and times.

Taking the example of a performance of *Hamlet* in Paris, Sartre says: "Hamlet is not here, he is not on the stage, he is in Denmark, hence far away from the *Comédie Française*" (p. 23). What is bothersome is that no distinction is made in this sentence between a fictional Denmark (to be imagined, and imaginary) and the geographical Denmark (to be imagined, but not imaginary). The latter is at a certain kilometric distance from Paris. If Hamlet is in this geographical Denmark at the time of a performance in Paris (or at any other historical time), he is an historical individual. And he should be closer to the historical spectators and actors if the performance takes place in Copenhagen.

Neither English nor French provides a special vocabulary, or a special affix to be added to nouns or verbs, for fiction. Thus it is that my remarks about characters and events in Sartre's plays will hardly differ stylistically from remarks about historical entities, though a semantic divergence is intended. A stylistic difference may be that, if "Caesar" names an historical individual, past tenses are appropriate (Caesar conquered Gaul so many years before he is said to have conquered Gaul), whereas a present tense is normal if "Caesar" names a fictional character in a play that is talked about. Similarly, I may simply write: "Sartre says in *Being and Nothingness,*" without bothering to historicize this ludic Sartre ("Sartre wrote in July 1942 in Paris"). The present tense in these cases is not an historical present, which indicates a more or less precise synchrony between the speaking event and the event spoken of. The present tense in these cases is rather what might be called a metatense.

Since what is essential in an essay is not a spatial and temporal logic, but nontemporal relations between concepts, I do not think it matters if there is an ambivalence in some of my remarks about Sartre (or myself). But a clear distinction between fictional and historical does matter in the case of texts to be basically interpreted as composing a fictional world. Historical, ludic, esthetic fields are supposed to be autonomous spatial and temporal fields. If there were spatial and temporal relations between them, we would be dealing with only one field.

A problem of interpretation may arise if the text uses words and phrases that a spectator, or reader, recognizes as names of singular historical entities: persons, nations, places, landmarks, dated historic events.

Actually, within the historical field, various contexts make such appellations refer to different entities. Several humans, dogs, cities, a military operation, a species of roses, a perfume, may receive one and the same name, or vice-versa. Aristotle used to be called the philosopher; we may call some particular philosopher a new Aristotle.

These remarks suggest a way in which a spectator, or reader, can transfer names of historical entities to fiction. Suppose that a city is named "Paris" in a drama, and that names like "Eiffel Tower," "Champs-Elysées," also appear. Let us extend the scope of antonomasia over the gap between historical and fictional. "Paris" may then be considered as the name of a class of cities, one historical, the others fictional. All these cities are similar, as befits a set, to the extent at least that details are given. But they are not one and the same city.

It is to be noted that what is said without inner contradiction about a city in a piece interpreted as fiction is axiomatic. An understanding of fiction as such involves a suspension of disbelief, and correlatively a suspension of belief. The Euclidean axiom of parallels is neither to be believed nor disbelieved. What may be a matter of belief, doubt, confirmation, disconfirmation, is a scientific application of a pure mathematical game to the historical field. A fictional detective imposes an axiomatic solution; an historical detective proposes a solution that may be believed or disbelieved, confirmed or disconfirmed. What is said about Paris in a piece I interpret as fiction may match what I believe about an historical city, as far as details are given in the fiction. But, in the case of the fictional city, the only verification that can be imagined is checking words printed in a copy of a book. This material volume is an historical entity. Two statements about the historical Paris may be incompatible. There may also be logical incompatibilities within a piece of fiction, but not between several pieces of fiction, nor between historiography (or geography) and pieces of fiction.

If a piece of fiction accumulates details which match what a reader, or spectator, believes he knows about singular historical individuals and places, the impression of similarity may turn to an impression of identity. Let me call "legendary" such confusions, or inextricable mixtures, between fictional and historical (this terminological move does not make it necessary for a legendary figure to be related to a hallowed past). Let me call "allegorical" a confusion between an individual and a class of individuals (men turned into an individual called Man), or between an individual and a philosophical concept. A failure to distinguish between one historical city and one fictional city would come under the head of legend. If the same thing occurs for several fictional cities and one historical city, the legend turns into an allegory. The term "myth" may be used to cover both legend and allegory.

In *What is Literature?*, Sartre opines that literary products should be aimed at an audience spatially and temporally close. If such is the case, one might surmise that an esthetic estrangement will be achieved if the historical setting is sufficiently distant. This relative distancing might have the effect of an "absolute" esthetic distance.

However, this is not what Sartre does in some of his plays. Furthermore, not only is it difficult to enforce the limitation of the potential audience in this way, it is also rather pointless, in view of the various interests and backgrounds of spectators and readers in the same place at the same time.

Some Frenchmen may not remember anything about the historical Julius Caesar. Those that remember something may have no particular interest in him, and may foresee no situation in which their vague memories would have a practical use. Their shadowy Julius Caesar should not interfere at all with a fictional Caesar. On the other hand, a specialist of Roman history may be bothered by a combination of similarities and dissimilarities between a fictional Caesar and his historical Caesar.

Someone may try to exploit the memories of his past experiences in a utilitarian way. He may also select details that he remembers, and transfer them to a fictional field if he writes a story. Or he may remain halfway, dreaming his past. To this extent, his past is legendary.

Historiographers are not content to ascertain physical facts, external happenings. They select, compose, link details they believe to be factual, with psychological surmises for instance. Such surmises can hardly be checked. Hence various legendary portraits of Napoleon, which constitute an allegorical figure if we lump them together.

It is not only in nocturnal dreams that fictional and historical domains are confused. Victor Hugo was a madman who believed he was Victor Hugo. We do not need to be afflicted with fame to legendize ourselves and each other with and without words. The radical distinction which is made in this essay between utilitarian (historical) existence and fictional (ludic or esthetic) existence is theoretical. In practice, it is sometimes quite clear; sometimes it is not. If it were always as clear as a distinction between a car and a saucepan, it would be otiose to stress it in theory.

Sometimes, Sartre makes a clear theoretical distinction between historical and fictional; sometimes he does not. For instance, he contends that "at the movies, we *are* the hero, we identify with him, we are headed toward disaster" (p. 88). Taken seriously, this declaration assumes illusion, and denies that the cinema can be an artistic medium, with its own means of isolating fictional worlds, thanks basically to the fantastic jumps and peculiar "eyesight" of cameras. I should prefer to say that, playfully, we identify with the cameras.

In *What is Literature?,* Sartre says: "We can safeguard literature only if we endeavor to demystify our audience" (*Situations,* II, 306). But, in *A Theatre of Situations,* he adds: "I deeply believe that a demystification must be mystifying in a sense . . . We must provide a countermystification. In order to do this, the theatre must fully exploit its sorcery" (p. 77). The idea behind this passage may be that a social dialectic has to proceed by myth and countermyth, and that a dramatist had better take part in it if he wants to make a hit (or a splash). But, on a more basic semantic level, it may be contended that dramatic art can, and should, isolate fiction as much as possible, instead of confirming mythical perspectives of interpretation. If this possibility is not taken advantage of, what point would there be in writing and performing dramas? An exploitation of dramatic "sorcery" may foster a confusion between historical and fictional existence. But it may just as well be aimed at the creation of entities that can exist without having to be supported by such a confusion.

A philologist may view Shakespeare's idiolect as part of an historical process called "English." But Hamlet did (does) not speak English at the beginning of the seventeenth century, nor Danish some time before. He speaks in a language which is not part of an historical *langue.* As Sartre suggests in *A Theatre of Situations,* the estrangement of fictional utterances from the daily medley is a matter of systematic stylization (selection, concentration). Actually, what linguists consider as a *langue,* either synchronically or diachronically, also involves a selection, but with different purposes, in particular that of turning some more or less widespread habits into rules.

PHILOSOPHICAL AND DRAMATIC

In a 1960 interview, Sartre said: "I think that today philosophy is dramatic . . . It is concerned with man, who is both an *agent* and an *actor,* who produces and plays his drama, as he lives the contradictions of his situation until his person explodes or his conflicts are solved . . . This is why the theatre is philosophical and philosophy is dramatic" (*Situations,* IX, 12-13).

This quotation illustrates several Sartrean tendencies: a tendency to privilege dramatic types of meaning; a tendency to generalize rashly (what is said would not apply to British and American philosophy, nor would it apply to the kind of philosophizing that was developing in France at the time, under the influence of Levi-Strauss, or of the later Heidegger, in particular); a tendency to characterize a period with traits that can also be found elsewhere (uses of theatrical synecdoches to picture the human condition are traditional); a tendency to be interested only in humans (human chauvinism) and to reduce human diversity to an allegorical figure (Lord Man); a strong Hegelian strain (talk about contradictions and syntheses, tendency to reduce gestural aspects to Romantic drama, leaving out farcical incongruities, stressed by Montaigne for instance); formulas that are often brilliant, but also hyperbolic (what is quoted talks about a philosophical topic, not about philosophical method and style; "philosophy is metadramatic" would thus be more appropriate, though the Hegelian aspect of the quotation suggests that the kind of philosophizing that is evoked might be dramatic in its very method).

Sartre's first major essay, *Being and Nothingness* (1943), pictures humans as actors, instead of just agents. This is already suggested by the formula: "Man is what he is not and is not what he is." Parodying Hamlet, one might say: "How to be and not to be, that is the question." The attempt to attribute some kind of being to nonbeing, which starts with Plato, will not be pursued here. Playing a critical game, I partly translate Sartre's terminology into mine (*traduttore tradittore*). I shall reduce "to be" and "to exist" to copulas. Saying "X is not" or "X does not exist" is incomplete. One should specify: "X does not exist as an A." Philosophical concepts (concepts of values, for instance) exist as concepts; scientific variables as variables, ludic roles as roles, esthetic characters as characters. Historical individuals have existed or will exist as such. Legendary and allegorical figures may even be said to exist as such, since these kinds of confusion do occur. My purpose is to break the spell of "being" and "existence."

Being and Nothingness dwells on *mauvaise foi* ("bad faith"). I translate this term as "self-hypocrisy." One of the etymological meanings of "hypocrite" is comedian. But, in the ordinary sense, we are hypocrites to the extent that we pretend not to be play-acting. And we often seem to be pretending that to ourselves. Hypocrisy (as distinct from candid play-acting) is inevitable, if we think it worthwhile to linger a little longer on this deplorable planet. A certain amount of self-hypocrisy is also inevitable. We have only one body, one nervous system, one set of words, to act and play-act. Playing fields, theatrical stages for instance, have to transfigure geographical space.

Sartre presents the human condition as ambiguous. The ambiguities, or confusions, of self-hypocrisy come under the head of what I call legend and allegory. We legendize ourselves and each other; playing and working are often inextricable mixtures. At times, some people may even seem to turn into allegories. They are identified with the mock-Platonic Ideas of the Mother, the Frenchman, the Revolutionary, the Artist, Man, Woman, Humanity. Other people are imitations.

Being and Nothingness chooses shame as the "original" experience of other persons. This basic shame is the awareness that one's own existence is unjustified. Hence activites aimed at self-justification. To be justified in our own eyes, we would need to believe that we are justified in the eyes of some chosen others (posterity in some cases, or some god).

Being and Nothingness thus differs from *Nausea,* in which existential shame is experienced by a solitary character, who feels his superfluity, his lack of *raison d'être,* in conjunction with material objects, and in opposition to esthetic entities (a song). In *Being and Nothingness,* it is others who can make us feel our incarnation as unjustified. And these others are exclusively human. Nonhuman animals are ignored; God is suggested, but rejected.

Thus, the picture of the human condition sketched in *Being and Nothingness* stresses features that dramatic art can exploit most conveniently. *Being and Nothingness* presents encounters with others as antagonistic, and shows how a dramatic dialectic of conflicts can be engineered. It eliminates nonhuman animals. Some of them can play; indeed, they may even appear to be able to distinguish between play-acting and deadly fight better than some humans. But they can hardly be recruited by a stage director. And they do not seem to be bothered by existential shame, an echo, in Sartre's philosophy, of the original sin. *Being and Nothingness* emphasizes our embodiment, not in contact with material things, but in relationships with others. It is their "glance" that incarnates us. It is they, rather than things, that can limit our freedom by challenging the meanings, the values, we want to give to our activities. Finally, if physical pain, fear, biological needs such as hunger, are mentioned, the emphasis is laid on less strongly or precisely embodied experiences: shame, indefinite anxiety, despair, feeling of responsibility, a desire to seduce others with gestures, especially verbal gestures.

Dwelling on self-hypocrisy, *Being and Nothingness* does not make a clear distinction between acting and play-acting, utilitarian and playful activities. It always talks of "being in the world," and the singular "the world" does not allow a distinction between the historical field and fictional fields, even on a theoretical level. At one point, it is said that "as soon as a man recognizes his freedom and wants to use it, whatever his anxiety may be, his activity is an activity of play" (*L'Etre et le Néant,* p. 669). I myself have noted that, characteristically, playful activities make the uncertainty of *their* future pleasant, while esthetic contemplation simply eliminates this uncertainty; at most, contemplation can distinguish between before and after. But *Being and Nothingness* makes no basic distinction between utilitarian, ludic, esthetic kinds of experiences, activities, domains. The three perspectives of interpretation I have distinguished to analyze the spectacle of a dramatic performance are thus given no philosophical basis.

What about a philosophical activity such as that undertaken by Sartre in writing *Being and Nothingness* ? A philosophical player may be thinking of other people, of possible readers for instance, while he is writing. But, to the extent that he is playing a philosophical role, he is not incarnated by them. He uses as partners and opponents other philosophical roles (*Being and Nothingness* names Hegel, Husserl, Heidegger, Plato), but he does not situate himself in relation to people called Herr Hegel or Herr Heidegger in the historical and utilitarian field. It is to name a composite ludic role that, in most sentences, I use "Sartre" in my essay. I treat it as a penname. If, by any chance, this essay of mine happens to be finished and published, it may provide some readers, if any, with material for a game of their own.

Empathy is required. But empathy covers antipathy as well as sympathy. Writing critically and singing in a choir are two different activities. In order to play, I need to compose my Sartre as an opponent as well as partner. In this respect, I approve of the stress that *Being and Nothingness* lays on antagonism. But it does not distinguish between a playful partner-opponent and a utilitarian ally-enemy (I do not need enemies, but I need opponents). Nor does it distinguish ludic understanding (philosophical, for instance) from utilitarian knowledge (scientific, for instance). Reminiscent of the opposition between mind and matter, that between man and thing rather suggests that knowledge of men is the business of philosophy. No doubt, human brains are still, to a large extent, refractory to scientific models and laws. But so are brains of nonhuman animals. And someone may empathize with a west wind more than with a human. In this case, the empathy should be poetic more than dramatic.

In his autobiographical essay *Les Mots* (*The Words*), published in 1964, Sartre adopts a critical attitude toward his role as writer, an attitude which, in some respects, is close to the one I adopt. For instance: "What I have just written is false. True. Neither true nor false, like everything that is written about madmen, about men. I have reported the facts as accurately as my memory allowed. But to what extent did I believe in my madness? . . . Acts themselves will not provide criteria, unless it is proved that they are not gestures, which is not always easy" (*Les Mots,* p. 61). "Gestures," here, appears to mean "mere gestures," "play-acting."

Indirectly, this passage tends to show that philosophizing, though it does make use of cognitive presupppositions, is not a utilitarian activity moved by cognitive goals, but a ludic activity which does not propose to reach and offer solutions to cognitive problems. Philosophy differs from fiction and from pure poetry. But its objective is similar in that a conceptual schema is not something that can be verified.

The model of human reality (and unreality?) offered in *Being and Nothingness* is not scientific (physiological). Philosophy is a defining game. The right to define is assorted with duties. For instance, one had better not give to "man" the same sense as to "pumpkin" (except on Halloween). This kind of game should be left to poets. But two philosophical definitions of the same word belonging to two essays are not contradictory. They are different.

How can one apply the Sartrean notion of bad faith? By sticking electrodes into brains? Philosophical concepts are not scientific variables like temperature and mass. Thanks to nonverbal instruments, science can apply mathematized models. Philosophy is stuck with words. I have only Sartre's printed words and my own words to discern identities and differences between what he means by *geste, mauvaise foi,* and what I mean by "gesture," "self-hypocrisy." I compose my Sartre; someone else will compose another.

From a utilitarian (cognitive) standpoint, these remarks are damning. From a ludic standpoint, diversity is interesting, incongruities may be amusing. But, if one insists on adopting a Hegelian role, free diversities must be reduced to contradictions, dramatic conflicts. This is the kind of cuisine that a Hegelian ogre can digest (synthesize).

Some ludic roles are anthropomorphic: roles in sports, anthropomorphic roles in a performed play. Writing an essay, a novel, a play, is not so physical. All the same, should not we say that those are human roles? Yes, if a certain definition of "human" is adopted, that of Sartre for instance, and if computers are not made to play philosophy as well as chess. The word "human" is used in my essay, but it is not part of my philosophical terminology.

In English or French, for obvious utilitarian reasons, it is customary to subordinate indications of fictional domains to indications of the historical domain. An historical man may be said to believe he is a bird, to have dreamed last night that he was a bird, to be playing the role of a bird in a comedy, or a philosophical role in a discussion or a book. Of course, I adopt this convention: I am not writing a pure poem. But this does not prevent me from putting historical and fictional on the same conceptual level. Likewise for utilitarian (cognitive and moral) and ludic-esthetic values. Including philosophical values.

Signs are what is experienced. And they are interpreted in various fundamental ways, which produce various sorts of signified entities. These modes of interpretation do not have to be rolled into one, nor even hierarchized, on the theoretical level. Each one has its depths, its strengths and weaknesses, its vision and blindness. Some experienced signs may be interpreted so as to signify a utilitarian anthropos in the historical field, a ludic anthropos in a playing field, an esthetic anthropos in an esthetic field.

I have stressed the metadramatic aspect of *Being and Nothingness.* But have Sartre's essays a directly dramatic aspect in their method and style?

I spoke of philosophical roles. Either assumed or ascribed to opponents, these roles are hardly dramatic. A "live" philosophical discussion may resemble a performance of an improvised farce. But this is because it lacks philosophical coherence. Philosophical dialogues, with fictional characters, have been written. But, even in Plato, they reveal that the composition of an exciting dramatic dialectic ill agrees with the composition of a conceptual schema.

Hegel may be viewed as having attempted to fuse (or confuse) a temporal logic and an intemporal (conceptual) logic. More precisely, I would adopt Sartre's suggestion that Hegelian "contradictions" are dramatic conflicts. This is why I chose the term "dialectic" to name dramatic kinds of composition. Drama happens to be the art that Hegel crowns.

However, Hegel does not consider his dialectic as something special to dramatic art or to dramatic snatches in the semantic jungle of daily life. He lumps together some details belonging to a broad historical period, sweeps the rest under the rug, and interprets these details in such a way as to compose a dialectic of individuated and even personified notions, above all Lord Spirit, in its successive avatars and metamorphoses. I am reminded of the *Roman de la Rose.* But, in this ironical medieval text, characters named Love, Reason, Pleasure, are presented as dreamed by an obviously fictional character: fiction to the second degree. On the contrary, Hegel pretends to historicize everything (except his own activity). Hence a comprehensive myth (legend plus allegory) designed to replace Christian myths.

Unlike *Being and Nothingness,* Sartre's *Critique of Dialectical Reason,* published in 1960, agrees to consider humans as an animal species, stresses needs rather than desires. Instead of concentrating on alienation by particular persons, it dwells on alienation by nonhuman factors, and by human groups. Tools appear bewitched, animated, when they turn against their users; and this "counterfinality" suggests a way in which a dramatist can give gestural import to props. The myth-countermyth dialectic of groups is analyzed, though not in these terms. Since Sartre does not grant a soul to a group apart from its members, each member has to be an allegorical incarnation of the group ("I" equals "We").

Like *Being and Nothingness, Critique of Dialectical Reason* may be called metadramatic in its outlook. And, like *Being and Nothingness,* it fails to distinguish, on the theoretical level, between the ludic and utilitarian elements that are mixed and confused in practice. The grouped individuals it talks about do not distinguish between a utilitarian allegiance (team of workers, army) and a playful allegiance (sports team). This lack of distinction may be called a religious tie. *Critique* adds allegory to legend. And yet a distinction between utilitarian enemies and ludic opponents should matter in Sartre's perspective: we are alienated by enemies, not by opponents. The former frustrate us (maim, jail, torture); the latter allow us to play, and enrich us. Thus my Sartre.

Neither *Being and Nothingness* nor *Critique* develop a temporal sequence. The second volume of the latter essay was to present various conflicts between human individuals and groups as constituting one big dialectical process labeled "History," replete with dramatic ironies. But like other books announced by Sartre, this second volume has not been published.

Instead of that, we have essays that bear on the evolution of particular people (Genet, Flaubert). They apply the Sartrean postulate that each man continually attempts to gather himself as a totality and is propelled from stage to stage by internal and external conflicts. Such essays are metadramatic, since they view their topic as a Romantic drama. To some extent, they are directly dramatic, for they adopt a chronological development and stick close to the standpoint attributed to the character undergoing metamorphoses. Though it could hardly be performed, the philosophical role assumes aspects of a dramatic monologue. To be noted in particular: a conjunction of Genet's slang with philosophical vocabulary.

The book on Genet (*Saint Genet Comédien et Martyr,* published in 1952) is a better example of the technique than the book on Flaubert. The latter is monstrously fat, while the former is only lengthy. Furthermore, the material extracted from Genet is better suited than the Flaubertian documents to the kind of plotting that Sartre undertakes. Actually, some of the characters in Genet's play *Le Balcon,* published in 1956, speak as if they had read Sartre's *Saint Genet.*

I have remained impressed by *Saint Genet.* It is quite original and ingenious. However, I am not tempted to adopt its method. As far as this particular essay of mine is concerned, it does not seem to me that Sartre's production, or his plays, would furnish a docile material. Actually, Sartre himself does not use the *Saint Genet* method in his autobiographical essay, *The Words.* In *The Words,* there are even passages that challenge the Sartrean postulate that the evolution of any man (in this case, Sartre himself) can honestly and comprehensively be reduced to a dialectical process impelled by nicely contrived contradictions.

More generally, I distrust the kind of styling that Sartre illustrates in *Saint Genet*, to the extent that an attempt to fuse narrative-dramatic and philosophical types of meaning generates allegories. I dislike allegorizing, except for ironical purposes. No doubt, there have to be narrative and gestural stylistic features in an essay (examples, explanations of moves); a set of axiomatic definitions is not enough. But, in my view, the purposes of these elements should be, not to compose one narration, one dramatic script, some *Roman de la Rose*, but to contribute to the extraction, formation, and articulation of concepts. Speaking about Genet, Sartre is not content to stress an allegorical and legendary aspect in Genet's writing, a religious aspect in his thinking. He also endorses them to some extent. For instance, in this enigmatic footnote:

> Either morals is a farce or it is a concrete totality which effects the synthesis of Good and Evil. For the Good without Evil is Parmenidean Being, i.e. Death; and Evil without the Good is pure Nothingness. To this objective synthesis correspond, as a subjective synthesis, the recovery of negative freedom and its integration into absolute freedom or freedom proper. It will be understood, I hope, that I am not talking about a Nietzschean transcendence of Good and Evil, but rather of a Hegelian *Aufhebung*. The abstract separation of these two notions simply expresses the alienation of man. But this synthesis, in the present historical situation, is impossible. So any morals which does not present itself explicitly as *impossible today* contributes to the alienation and mystification of men. (*Saint Genet Comédien et Martyr,* p. 177)

The passage illustrates at least two Sartrean propensities: the pretension, or pretence, to speak in the name of all contemporary interpreters (yet, your picture of our-time may differ from mine; and what is so special about our present historical situation as far as what is talked about is concerned?); also a Hegelian taste for "totalities," "syntheses," "concrete universals." To me, a concrete universal can but be an individuation of a set of individuals or of a philosophical concept, i.e. an allegorical figure. The use of capitalized nouns in the singular contributes to a confusion between names of individuals and names of concepts.

"Good" and "evil," or, better, "moral values and antivalues," may be used to name the two poles of a concept. This bipolarity is not a dramatic conflict between characters or within a character. In practice, of course, there will be conflicts, since a concept is not a measurable variable, and since various people, within the same culture or not, may define and apply "good" and "evil" differently.

What is meant by "synthesis of Good and Evil" remains a mystery to me, like Blake's marriage of heaven and hell. I read somewhere that Zeus was the son of Cronos and Gaia; but, regarding the union of Good and Evil, I have no idea of the synthetic egg that would be hatched.

Sartre speaks of an historical impossibility. I would prefer to speak of the semantic impossibility of fusing individuals and concepts in a way that would not be a confusion. Of course, I recognize that such confusions occur. Inevitably. Cultural and countercultural loudspeakers, fashions and cants, blow them up. Otherwise, philosophizing would be pointless. I cannot claim that there is no trace of allegorizing in my essay beyond ironical passages. At least, it is not my purpose. In my view, allegorizing adds superfluously to semantic alienation and mystification.

In the quoted passage, Good is identified with Being and Death. The God of medieval theologians is identified with Good and Being (but not Death). Some theologians hint that they are speaking allegorically. Still, they cling to a personification of what is divine. Romantically, Sartre prefers the word "Man" (*l'Homme*) to the word "God." "Man, oh not men," exclaims Shelley, not content to allegorize winds and clouds. Man is the major allegorical figure in Sartrean language.

The short essay *Of Rats and Men* (*Des Rats et des Hommes*) lays bare the device by using the singular *l'Homme* as the name of *the* personified ideal value, and substituting "rats" for "men" (animal species): "This absence is Man, our tyrant. We are unmasked: rats preyed upon by Man" (*Situations,* IV, 60).

Sartre writes as if he could, or wanted to, enlist every reader under a banner marked "we." I assume that, outside comatose states, every human, or "rat," or "donkey," needs dreams, stars, carrots or pieces of cheese, in order to live with himself and keep himself going in a certain direction. But some may be content with various small carrots, adapted to circumstances, while others may attempt to synthesize these carrots into one big Santa Claus. This is the way Sartre often acts, play-acts. But what about the daily life of the now dead

Sartrean "rat"? Besides, if ideals are turned into one personified figure, why should this figure be given the name "Man," rather than "Abracadabra"? Charles de Gaulle (the troubadour, not to be confused with the general and statesman) calls "France" his faraway princess, so far away that the estrangement is esthetic. This fictional lady must have been particularly beautiful when April was there and the general in London.

WHY FICTION?

Four kinds of values, or goals, may be distinguished. A cognitive activity attempts to modify (confirm, disconfirm, erase, add to) what is believed to be known. A moral activity attempts to terminate, alleviate, prevent some suffering. The goal of a ludic activity is to enjoy the activity for its own sake. Esthetic values differ from ludic values as contemplation (repose) differs from activity. Esthetic values alone are contemplative.

According to interpreters and circumstances, these kinds of goals are more or less compatible and incompatible. Someone may bicycle for pleasure, fall down a ravine, be killed. This is morally good from the standpoint of his enemies, also from his standpoint if he wishes to die, but not from the standpoint of those who rely on him. A biological inquisitor may be moved by cognitive goals. He may even enjoy the art of what, in other people's eyes, would be the torture of victims, human or not. Earning a living may appear to him as a sufficient moral goal. Someone may enjoy writing for its own sake. If he also thinks of communicating the result, this perspective is utilitarian. The two perspectives are not always incompatible.

The essay on ethics that Sartre announces in *Being and Nothingness* has not been published. All I can gather from what is said at the end of *Being and Nothingness* is that an authentic moral perspective would involve the recognition that freedom is the source of values, in other words that goals are chosen and have to be chosen. By itself, this recognition orients one at most toward a ludic perspective: enjoying the exercise of freedom for its own sake. From my standpoint, an authentic moral attitude would imply, as a precondition, a distinction between moral goals and others, while self-hypocrisy attempts to confuse them. But would this distinction satisfy a Sartrean taste for totalities?

This taste manifests itself in a 1960 interview: "If literature is not *everything*, it is not worth one hour of trouble" (*Situations,* IX, 15). Sartre often gives the impression that, for him, anything must be everything or nothing, or better, everything and nothing. This, I suppose, would fit a medieval God's point of view. In the same interview, Sartre adds, still speaking about literature: "Its beauty is to want to be everything, not vainly to seek after beauty. Only a *whole* can be beautiful." But a detached esthetic whole (*un tout*) is not everything (*tout*). I would have again to conjure up a medieval God, or a Platonic Engineer, to turn everything into an esthetic whole.

In *What is Literature?*, an essay, or manifesto, written in 1947, Sartre might appear to want texts to have the four kinds of virtues I distinguished. In the eyes of a Sartrean reader, a text would be totally good if it afforded him playful pleasure on first reading, contemplative pleasure on rereading, and if he judged it to provide true information and to have benefic repercussions on all readers' practical behavior.

What is Literature? discards poetry. This move seems at first to make sense, since Sartre is thinking of pure poetry, not of "lyrical poetry," a label which may apply to short versified narratives or texts that sound like dramatic monologues.

As likely candidates, one might think of texts of scientific vulgarization, technical handbooks, sociological enquiries, reportages, exposures, exhortations, that a reader would judge well-written, credible and accurate, effective and benefic.

However, the examples given in *What is Literature?* show that Sartre is thinking primarily of fiction, and secondarily of essays, such as the one he is writing. This must be because dramas, films, novels, as he conceives them, offer the greatest amount of similitudes with daily living. Everyday uses of language mostly offer narrative and gestural elements. Texts of fiction compose spatio-temporal worlds, build characters somewhat in the way we concoct ourselves and others in daily living. Pure philosophy, on the contrary, arranges concepts in an intemporal (which does not mean "eternal") field. And pure poetry atomizes, disperses personification: fleeting animation is found indiscriminately in mixed human and nonhuman poetic evocations.

A question already examined arises again. The esthetic world composed by a text of fiction risks losing its detachment from the historical field if similarity fosters the illusion of identity. Thus, the imaginary world would lose its esthetic integrity. And a mystification would be produced, as far as cognitive virtues, hence some moral issues, are concerned.

La Fontaine's fable, *The Raven and the Fox*, ends with a cognitive proverb coupled with moral advice: beware of flatterers because they live at the expense of the flattered. We do not need a short story to be told that. The story is enjoyable in itself; but story and maxim do not constitute one esthetic world. Take off the maxim. What is the utilitarian significance of the story? That we should beware of foxes that speak in French verse, if we have stolen a piece of cheese? Or that robbers should and will be robbed? Or that it is proper to pay for services received (flattery in this case)? Or that quadrupeds are smarter than bipeds?

Critics can extract all kinds of utilitarian significance from novels, films, dramas, which are much longer than La Fontaine's fable. Such large pieces of fiction can make characters proffer proverbs and maxims. But such utterances do not have to be taken for scientific laws or philosophical axioms. And it is dramatically better to have characters proverbialize at cross-purposes.

Sartre does not want, or does not simply want, characters to reflect on life in general. He wants the significance of pieces of fiction to have a special bearing on a contemporary situation. This requirement should make the relevance of a piece of fiction fade quickly. It may also threaten esthetic integrity when and where the text is read or performed for the first time.

Above all, it appears absurd to resort to fiction in order to inform, except to the extent that censorship and libel laws make it unavoidable or prudent: what is told is true; the names have been changed to protect the innocent, the guilty, and the legal author. Sartre's totalitarian taste does not go as far as totalitarian regimes. Yet, it is a totalitarian regime that makes it most unavoidably proper to resort to fiction in order to suggest what is hidden, instead of directly presenting what someone believes to be fact, with source of information spelled out. Besides, a totalitarian regime should make the audience more homogeneous. And Sartre deplores the heterogeneity of his prospective audience in the France of 1947. This heterogeneity makes for diverse interpretations and reactions, and reduces the probability of practical repercussions.

(Sartre does try to delimit his prospective audience by relying on a simple cut between bourgeois and workers, and generously abandoning the latter to the Communist Party. This gratuitous, and restful, decision allows him to view his critical role as that of an antibourgeois bourgeois. I myself would think that Sartre's serious readers have been mostly teachers and students in the humanities. But, in any case, whatever the merits of the bourgeois-worker dichotomy may have been from an economic or political standpoint, I distrust its application to the tastes, attitudes, expectations of readers of fiction.)

What is Literature? speaks of "unveiling the world." But this hyperbolic metaphor may have nothing to do with what I call cognitive goals and virtues. Let us remember that, in *The Words*, Sartre reduces what is said "about men, about madmen," to a neither-true-nor-false status, i.e. to fiction. A novel, a drama, a film, like a philosophical essay, rely on what is believed to be known about the historical field, about a contemporary situation in particular. But they are not expected to confirm, disconfirm, erase, add to, cognitive beliefs, by providing new evidence. A reader may wonder whether this or that detail in a piece of fiction can be translated as information or misinformation. But, if he is interested in knowledge, rather than legend, it is not other pieces of fiction that will provide him with further evidence.

So, what pieces of fiction could offer would be various ways of comprehending certain experiences, not factual knowledge about "the world." The same may be said, not only about philosophy, but also pure poetry, so that Sartre's dismissal of pure poetry now appears unjustified. In view of his temperament and past experiences, a reader may find more illumination in ten lines of Apollinaire than in thousands of pages of Balzac or Tolstoy. And it may not matter whether the text was recently published or not. Someone may find more in Schopenhauer, Hume, or even Plato, than in Sartre. He may find in Sartre an interesting opponent. He may use Sartre as an agitator, a catalyst, or he may dismiss him as merely agitated, a dud. Perspectives of understanding do not have the cumulative aspect of science.

In *What is Literature?*, Sartre says: "The task of criticism has become *total*, it involves the whole man" (*Situations,* II, 310). I wish that he had made his own attitude critical enough to bear on his uses of the adjective *total*. In any case, there is no tabula rasa. Any kind of thinking has to rely on some beliefs, or prejudices, on some postulates, on some words in order to analyze the meaning of others. Basically, it has to rely on uninterpreted non-sense. But what I want to point out right now is that a perspective of interpretation, were it only a poetic atmosphere, is critical of another, not because it brings evidence tending to prove that the other is false, but because it contributes to relativizing it. Plato may be used to relativize Hegel, Schopenhauer to relativize Sartre. What is deep and important for someone will be superficial and immaterial for his next-door neighbor. Philosophy, poetry, fiction, offer various perspectives. You can take your pick, choose what suits you as partner and opponent.

This conception of philosophy, poetry, fiction, does not prevent them from having some moral bearing. Philosophizing, as I see it, can be metacognitive and metamoral, rather than a directly cognitive and moral activity (informing, recommending a particular moral action). Yet the way a philosopher isolates moral values from others is already a commitment; for instance, if he says that pain, not death, is an evil; or if he says that fairness is a ludic, rather than moral, virtue. Philosophy proposes hypothetical examples. Fictional situations in novels and dramas may be interpreted in this way, as well as enjoyed in themselves.

In *What is Literature?*, Sartre adds these words to his evocation of a theatre of situations: "It is to be wished that literature become entirely moral and problematic, like this new theatre. Moral, not moralizing: let it simply show that man is *also* value, and that the question he asks are always moral" (*Situations*, II, 313).

Thus, Sartre implicitly distinguishes between literature and straight propaganda, moral exhortations. But the metamoral perspective that he proposes tends to restrict the field of moral goals, as well as sources, to anthropomorphic creatures, and, on the other hand, to view any kind of question as moral. This is not the way I would delimit a metamoral perspective. Others may be inclined to delimit it in a Sartrean way.

I also wonder whether the terms of a moral problem can be clearly laid down within a drama, without philosophical pointers. Of course, characters may philosophize. But it is difficult to integrate such philosophizing dramatically; and a reader, or spectator, is free to decide that what this or that character says does not correctly indicate the moral, or metamoral, significance of the play.

I have spoken of a diversity of perspectives offered by various texts published at the same time or not. Sartre prefers to speak of totalities. A set of literary texts published synchronically would be "the synthetic and often contradictory totality of what a period has been able to produce for its enlightenment" (*Situations*, II, 311).

I have noted that Sartre contends that, in order to demystify, dramas must provide a countermystification. This is in accord with his presentation of characters as myths: "Hamlet is an individual, but he is above all a myth" (p. 327). Instead of considering characters and situations as fictional entities similar to some persons and historical situations, spectators would confuse historical and fictional domains (legend), and would also confuse general and particular (allegory). This may very well occur. But, if a global mission is to be conferred on philosophy, poetry, and fiction, it should be, in my view, to contribute to vigilance. By "vigilance," I do not mean absence of dreams (this would be self-destructive), but recognition of dreaming as such.

By forcing various texts into a totality, Sartre turns literature into an allegorical figure. Often, though not always, in *What is Literature?*, his uses of singulars ("literature," "the reader," "the writer") allegorize. I am afraid *littérature engagée* might be translated as "engaged to allegorical figures." Lady Literature is engaged to Lord Man.

Practical efficacy often demands that individuals should be grouped. Sometimes, the situation is such that a mythical confusion between individual and group may be judged by someone a necessary or useful drug ("Black is beautiful"). It might be contended that Sartre turns the variety of texts, readers, writers, into allegories in order to unite his fellow-writers, so that their production may constitute a critical literature that would act as a global countermyth.

Thus, the critical mission that Sartre advocates would stop short of exposing mythical thinking itself. The trouble with myths and countermyths, when they are effective, is that they make it difficult to distinguish between going forward, backward, and round (a 1979-1980 example: Iran). Furthermore, as far as Sartre's own enterprise is concerned, what could be said in favor of this tactic from the standpoint of efficacy?

It is fairly easy to view French writers, concentrated in Paris, as a totality. In *What is Literature?,* Sartre pictures these Parisian writers, at least the best-known or most agitated ones, as characters in a farce. One might also use the image of writhing interwined snakes in a pit. These writers are more interested in short-term alliances and hostilities, on the personal level or that of coteries, than in the task of plotting a global countermyth. No doubt, since 1947, and especially since 1968, quite a few have talked of *contestation.* *Décrypter* and *transgresser* have relayed the Sartrean *dévoiler* and *dépasser.* But *contestations* have remained intramural bickering. Concerning readers, I should make the following assumptions:

1. As Sartre himself notes, the audience is heterogeneous. There is no united ideology instilled into readers, against which a concerted effort could be directed. Since 1947, myths have tended to disperse into various incohesive and transitory slogans.

2. Through technology, physics and chemistry have an impact that literature cannot match. (The Hegelian dialectic may be seen as an attempt to rescue philosophy from scientific threats.)

3. Theatre-goers are very few, readers of fiction few. The cinema draws

more and television, not considered by Sartre in 1947, many more.

4. A piece of fiction that is worth thinking about needs to be reread. How many people have the time or taste to reread critically?

5. Novels and plays that draw the largest audience are most often pieces that a self-respecting critic or historiographer would refuse to talk about. There may be no overlap between the texts read by two persons.

6. People who are likely to read recent texts that are talked about in academic circles are also likely to read older texts. This dispersion blurs the historical perspective.

It is a postulate of cognitive thinking that the historical field is one: we are not going to check in one world what has been asserted in and about another. So, it must be assumed that any event has repercussions, for instance reading a text of Sartre. But how can these repercussions, regarding a social situation, or a particular reader, be isolated and tested?

In *Being and Nothingness,* Sartre lays down the theoretical principle that each man is responsible for the whole world. In a way, yes, since the historical field is one. But this principle of total responsibility is equivalent to fatalism. My actions, my very thoughts about responsibility and fatalism, are theoretically part of a system in which each event signals (determines), and is signalled by, all the others, past *and* future. Practically, we don't know. Ignorance allows and forces us to experience guesses and decisions. An omniscient being would be perfectly impotent. He, or rather it, could not experience activities as such.

In theory, each event is "unique." Uniqueness can be thought, but as one pole of a concept whose other pole would be anythingness. This possibility shows the privilege of philosophical thinking, a privilege assorted with drawbacks. Uniqueness is experienced *through* events, individuals (even a speck of dust); but I cannot think the uniqueness *of* an event, since it is a member of the class of events. Thoughts and words circumscribe individuals with intersecting generalities, and link them with proverbs (dialectical relations for instance) and scientific laws: whenever an event of type X happens, it is followed by an event of type Y. Causality is the limit of probability.

What causalistic or probabilistic knowledge can I claim regarding the repercussions of Sartre's writings on historical situations and particular individuals, for instance myself? I cannot set up experimental conditions and make chosen factors vary, for instance remove my readings of Sartre and observe what happens (would have happened) to me. I am what I am, was what I was, shall be what I shall be. Impeccable tautologies. Impeccably useless. Except as a reminder. All I can say is that Sartre seems to have been the source of the vogue of a few words in some circles for some time. Words, not ideas. Verbal gestures.

How did Sartre himself estimate his influence? In 1960, as he was asked what things he thought his writings had contributed to changing, he said: "Not one. Since my youth, I have experienced total powerlessness" (*Situations,* IX, 25). The adjective "total" simplifies matters. I do not doubt Sartre's sincerity; but, at another time, he may have answered differently and just as sincerely. Besides, should I not consider this declaration simply as one of the things that are said "about men, about madmen," and that are "neither true nor false"?

Let me add this excerpt from a 1970 interview: "I wrote exactly the contrary of what I wanted to write" (*Situations,* IX, 134). Does this mean that his dramas and novels are at odds with his theory of *littérature engagée?* Or does this mean that his theory of literature itself is at odds with what he wanted to say? Does this mean that the bubbly fame which propelled him and Camus into roles of Parisian gurus toward 1944, and which, in my opinion, warped Sartre's line of development, and even more that of Camus, resulted, from Sartre's point of view in 1970, in a complete inversion of what he wanted to say, or thought he had to say?

Noting that Sartre is fond of dialectical reversals and dramatic ironies, we might wonder whether, in *What is Literature?,* he recommended a deliberately committed literature so as to trigger an opposite reaction (which, to some extent, did occur), hence a deliberately disengaged literature. Including an opposite reaction on the part of a playwright named Sartre?

Actually, what can be drawn from Sartre's various writings cannot be reduced to neat agreements or oppositions. To a great extent, when he talks about himself, Sartre shows us the other side of the coin: what his ludic role discarded. But not exactly that. There are overlaps between his writings. Big and small. There are consonances and discrepancies.

I shall compare aspects of Sartre's dramas with details in his other writings. I do not want to present his plays, either as perfect illustrations of his theorizing or in perfect opposition: as far as technique is concerned, *What is Literature?* and *A Theatre of Situations* remain very vague, and Sartre's plays are a fairly diverse bunch. Nor shall I try to clothe the chronological sequence of their production in dialectical garb.

PART II

PRACTICE

Note: In each section, unless otherwise indicated, page numbers refer to the text of the play to which the section is devoted. The editions that have been used are indicated in the bibliography.

BARIONA (1940)

This short drama (legendarily) takes place in Judea, the night of the birth of Christ. Lelius, a Roman administrator, tells Bariona, the chief of destitute villagers, that taxes have been raised. Bariona advises his men to obey. He has no hope for the village, which loses its young men to the city. He wants the village to die. Bariona's wife announces that she is pregnant. Bariona wants her to have an abortion. Then he asks God to give him a sign, if He wants the people of the village to continue to procreate. An angel announces the birth of Christ. Everybody leaves for Bethlehem, except for Bariona, who refuses to believe in the sign. A sorcerer predicts the life and death of Christ. Bariona rushes to Bethlehem to kill the newborn child. But he relents and finally accepts a lesson of courage and hope: "We men, who have been created in God's image, stand beyond our suffering to the extent that we are like God" (p. 624). He is told to let his own child live, in spite of what he will have to go through: "He alone will have to deal with his suffering and he will do with it just what he will like, for he will be free" (p. 626). Bariona sacrifices himself and other men to allow the Holy Family to flee.

*   *   *

A Christmas play, *Bariona* was written while Sartre was a prisoner of war, with the approval of priests in the same camp. Fellow-prisoners were the actors and the audience. The play was published much later.

In this crude exercise, the precise Christian topic is not to be taken too seriously. It is treated in such a way as to offer something to believers and unbelievers alike. Sartre does not seem to have been interested in the Father and the Son. The Holy Ghost is another matter. Like other philosophers, he is interested in the mystery of Incarnation. But he does not concentrate it in a particular historical, or legendary, event. Theoretically, any human being is Christ. A concentration appears when an allegorical figure christened "Man" is substituted for various human beings.

One of the interesting aspects of *Bariona* is the apparition of an optimistic notion of freedom. The experience of freedom would be so strong that it would allow any human being to prevail over his suffering whatever it might be.

This voluntaristic conception is developed in *Being and Nothingness* (1943) in less rosy terms, since this essay stresses the anxious experience of having to decide, coupled with the principle of total responsibility. However, the principle that one is responsible for the whole "world" may turn in practice into the impression of being responsible for nothing in particular.

In *Critique of Dialectical Reason,* Sartre shifts the stress from freedom to the correlative notion of situation. And, in *The Words,* the philosopher of responsibility dwells on the levity, the frivolity of a daily Sartre. An exaggeration perhaps: Sartre is fond of hyperboles. All I can say is that, in his writings, there is levity in the way (my) Sartre uses words sometimes. For instance, hyperboles.

The texts of fiction that Sartre had published before he wrote *Bariona* were narrative. The short stories collected in *The Wall* are ironical. The philosophical novel *Nausea* is sarcastic and pessimistic in a Proustian way: the only activity that, rather dubiously, the protagonist considers worthwhile at the end is writing a piece of fiction. He will be "saved" in his ludic role, through the construction of an esthetic world. Daily life is abandoned to a nauseous lack of *raison d'être.*

In *Bariona,* a pessimistic perspective (suffering should not be perpetuated) turns to an optimistic perspective. We may be responsible for others, especially if we procreate, but they are or will become responsible for their own existence (at what age?). So, responsibility is passed on, all the more conveniently since everybody is assumed to be able to triumph over his suffering (and that of others). It may be recalled that France, unlike Germany, had a very low birthrate in the nineteen thirties.

*   *   *

Communal living in a prison camp (not a concentration camp; or a penitentiary), perhaps without much friction, and the particular circumstances of the performance provided Sartre with the idea of a united audience, the absence of which he acknowledges in *What is Literature?* (1947), also in this passage, which refers to the 1940 performance of *Bariona* :

> I understood what the theatre should be: a great collective and religious phenomenon. Of course, I benefited from exceptional circumstances; it is not every day that your audience is united by a great common interest, a great loss, or a great hope. Usually, a theatrical audience is composed of very diverse elements: a big businessman is seated beside a traveling salesman or a teacher, a man beside a woman, and each spectator has his own particular concerns. Yet this situation is a challenge for a playwright: he must create his audience, fuse all these disparate elements into a single

unity by evoking what concerns everybody at a certain time in a given community. (*Un Théâtre de Situations,* p. 62)

I wonder whether the best example of a "great collective and religious phenomenon" would not be a Nazi rally in Nuremberg. Hitlerian "forgers of myths" had great success in making their audience uniform, and incitng spectators to "participate" and "commune" as actors. It was thanks to the success of this "theatre of cruelty" that Sartre got a ready-made "religious" audience in 1940.

In *Critique of Dialectical Reason* (1960), he presents groups as "fraternities through terror," and hatred of antigroups. Theatrical spectacles can be made part of this socioreligious dialectic. But they cannot provide the stick, the "secular arm."

It is often said that the theatre started from religious ceremonies. So it managed to get away. Why make it turn back? What can preserve its autonomy as an art, as a spectacular sport, is not a common interest and hope of the sort that Sartre alludes to, but an interest in the peculiarities of the art, an appreciation of techniques, a hope that a new play will be sound, and perhaps even bring something new in this respect.

Beyond that why not accept a diversity of sensibilities, past experiences, types of understanding, tastes, distributed in a way that does not match social categories? *Being and Nothingness* discards the notion of a human nature. *Critique* speaks of a human species. *The Words* recognizes temperaments. I agree with the latter two essays.

When someone reads, he can adopt the pace he likes; he does not risk being bothered by actors; he can return to page 20 after reading page 40, and pause to reflect. If he attends a performance of a play, or showing of a film, he is robbed of these privileges. But, for a dramatically oriented temperament, a ludic and esthetic conversion of sight and hearing will be appreciated as more than a compensation. As I see it, the purpose of the variety of ludic uses of words, and of particular products, is to allow various sensibilities to pierce through cultural and countercultural screens.

One play, like one novel, or essay, may offer different things to different spectators, or readers. It does not have to make interests and reactions uniform, in order not to be a flop. It may be contended, however, that a playwright has to try to channel reactions more imperiously than a novelist or essayist. For, during a performance, spectators react to one another. A dramatist would have to produce some kind of contagion.

The success of *En Attendant Godot* opened a breach for the plays I shall mention in the conclusion. Was this success partly due to a sprinkling of Christian baits, or contagious germs, to which spectators and reviewers thought it culturally proper to react? Did Sartre count on an irate show of the reviewer Mauriac to bring spectators to the first performances of *The Devil and the Good Lord*?

The Christian bait must have been superfluous in the case of *Bariona.* The prisoners must have welcomed a temporary substitution of a playing field for their Platonic cave. Beyond the vague virtue of a comforting drug, what significance would they draw from the play?

Let us suppose that they equated the Romans in the play with the Germans in their case. Bariona's situation remains quite different from theirs. At the end of the play, Bariona decides to undertake a delaying action against the Romans which should bring death to him and his companions. I suppose Sartre's intention was not to encourage his fellow-prisoners to start a rebellion against the German guards. Sensibly, they stayed put; some of them attempted to escape individually.

The play makes a definite plea in favor of procreation. There was a postwar baby boom in France. But I have no figures showing the number of children fathered by the spectators of *Bariona* in relation to the national average. As for Sartre himself, I think he said (he thought) he had not fathered any.

THE FLIES (1943)

In act I, using the pseudonym of Philebus, Orestes arrives, with his preceptor, in his native town, Argos, on the eve of the day when the dead are evoked and are supposed to come back to torment the living. Aegisthus, who has been in power since he killed Agamemnon, has generalized his own crime and instituted a cult of public repentance. A traveler, who calls himself Demetrios, and who seems to have been following Orestes, explains to him that the gods thought it advisable to turn the crime to "the benefit of moral order" (p. 110). They sent swarms of flies as a "symbol." It is hinted that Demetrios is something else than a mere mortal; the preceptor is struck by the resemblance of his magnificent beard with that of a statue of Jupiter. In veiled words, Demetrios-Jupiter warns Philebus-Orestes not to interfere with the state of affairs in the city, which is dear to the gods, and he gives Orestes a magic formula to get rid of the flies if they bother him. Orestes tells his preceptor that he is dissatisfied with the kind of freedom, the detached wisdom, that the latter has taught him: "How free I am! What a superb absence my soul!" (p. 121). He does not belong anywhere. He dreams of an act which would give him citizenship among the Argives; he dreams of appropriating their memories, their terrors, their hopes, in order to fill his empty heart, even if he had to kill his own mother. Enters Electra, who expresses her hatred and impotent revolt to Philebus. Clytemnestra joins them. She too confides in the stranger (who is her son). In Electra's words, she practices with him the national game of public confession. The queen rebukes her daughter: "Anyone can spit in my face, call me a criminal and a prostitute. But nobody has the right to judge my remorse" (p. 138). Philebus-Orestes announces to Demetrios-Jupiter that he has changed his mind: he will not leave the city.

In act II, Electra creates a scandal at the ceremony, and tries to persuade the Argives to stop their comedy of remorse. But Jupiter intervenes: the rock which obstructs the cave of the dead rolls away. Orestes discloses his identity to his sister. He hesitates about the course to follow, prays to Jupiter to give him a sign that he should leave. Jupiter complies, but the result is contrary to his expectations. Orestes claims his independence: "Nobody can give me orders now . . . You are *my* sister, Electra, and this city is *my* city" (p. 178). Jupiter warns Aegisthus that Orestes is planning to kill him. But Aegisthus is tired of the role he has been playing: he does not defend himself. Orestes then kills Clytemnestra, while Electra is showing signs of weakening.

In act III, the flies have been metamorphosed into the Furies. They watch Orestes and Electra, who have taken refuge in the temple of Apollo. Jupiter offers Orestes and Electra to reign over Argos. All they have to do is repent and preserve the cult of repentance in the city. Electra gives in, but Orestes refuses to deny what he did: "You are the king of gods, Jupiter, the king of stones and stars, the king of the waves on the sea. But you are not the king of men" (p. 232). Jupiter had already told Aegisthus: "Once freedom has exploded in the soul of a man, the gods can do nothing against him any longer" (p. 201). Jupiter accepts his defeat, and leaves. Orestes makes a speech to the Argives: he (symbolically) takes upon himself their failings, their remorse, their anxieties; he deserves to be their king, but he will not sit on the throne that Jupiter offered him. All he wants is to rid the Argives of the flies. Then he leaves, followed by the Furies.

*   *   *

The Flies was first performed in Paris, in 1943, during the German Occupation. At the time, it was almost inevitable that the audience should liken the behavior of Orestes to the activities of the Resistance, the reign of Aegisthus to the regime imposed by the Vichy government and the Germans. And yet the resemblances are vague and tenuous; otherwise the play could not have been performed. The interpretation of the 1940 disaster as punishment was exploited at one time by the Vichy government; but the repentance game assumes much greater importance in the play. "Freedom" is a word which is stressed in *The Flies*. But it does not mean a liberation from a foreign army. As in *Being and Nothingness,* the experience of freedom is the experience of making a decision, or the experience of having to make a decision and being responsible for choosing goals, for deciding what one should do. In an article about the Occupation years, Sartre wrote: "Never have we been so free" (*Situations,* III, 11). He meant that the situation was such that it sharpened the sense of having to choose a fundamental course of action. Actually, most Frenchmen must have been blissfully unaware of that. They simply tried to adjust.

The difference between the situation of Orestes and that of a Frenchman during the Occupation should also be noted. Orestes is a stranger to the city. He could leave without hindrance, and his decision to kill Aegisthus and Clytemnestra entails no physical danger to him, only the psychological threat of remorse. And there is no army to protect Aegisthus, who lets himself be killed without any resistance. Besides, what contemporary significance could the audience recognize in the family relationships, especially in the fact that Orestes is the son of the murdered king, the legitimate heir to the throne?

                    *   *   *

The Flies is the play in which echoes of *Being and Nothingness* are most noticeable. Recalling the moment of his decision, Orestes exclaims: "Suddenly, freedom swooped down on me and took hold of me; nature jumped back . . . And there was nothing left in heaven, neither Good nor Evil, and nobody could give me orders" (p. 234).

Freedom, more precisely the experience of deciding or having to decide, is described like a visitation of the Holy Ghost. Because of its suddenness, the decision is experienced as an inspiration; it is as if it happened to Orestes, instead of Orestes making it happen. It should be recalled that, in *Being and Nothingness,* man is presented as consciousness of being, rather than as conscious being. Consciousness (which may be equated with the spirit) is somehow impersonal. The ego is an object, it is the object of reflexive consciousness. The ego is part of "nature." Consciousness is opposed to nature as nothingness to being. Hence the phrase: "Nature jumped back." Hence also the assertion that Jupiter is the king of stones and stars, but not the king of men, in so far as they experience decisions, projects. When Orestes says: "I *am* my freedom (p. 233), he does not refer to the ego as object, but to subjectivity: he assumes the decision which took place in him, he coincides with it, maintains it. But the narrative shadow of his verbal gesture does localize what is talked about, as well as the speaker, somewhere, at a certain time.

The words of Orestes evoke experiences in which a decision somehow takes place impersonally. Later, it is realized that we have made a decision, embarked on a course of action. In this respect, the few words Orestes says about his experience might be added to, and counterbalance, the long passage in *Nausea* in which the protagonist, Roquentin, analyzes his experience of unjustified, superfluous existence. There is something mystical about both experiences. They challenge linguistic forms, in particular uses of the first person pronoun. They stress the mysteries of incarnation in two ways: passivity and activity.

Being and Nothingness distinguishes consciousness (and conscience) from ego. The short essay *Of Rats and Men* would support a different view: a pluralistic conception of consciousness, in the tradition of the bundle theory of the self. Internal egos may be pictured, for instance, as cameras, or spies, whose perspectives intersect. A state of consciousness is a common zone. This is only one image; others might be used for various kinds of experience: as far as types of experience are concerned, only images can be used. This conception would have the advantage of leaving room for subconscious and unconscious zones of experience, which the schema chosen in *Being and Nothingness* has to reject summarily. And it would have the advantage of avoiding singular forms ("consciousness," "the ego," "the Unconscious"), that I suspect of fostering allegories.

The suddenness of the decision reported by Orestes corresponds to the way temporality is analyzed in *Being and Nothingness*. Unlike Bergsonian duration, Sartrean temporality is discontinuous. Projecting itself into the future, human reality freezes the past, turns it into a springboard. The situation determines the conditions of a choice, not what is chosen. The situation may be tight; it may permit only a choice between ineffectual attitudes; yet human consciousness is choice under any circumstances. When Jupiter tells Orestes that he will have to praise the freedom of a prisoner in chains (p. 225), he cites a case which is also mentioned in *Being and Nothingness*. *Critique of*

Dialectical Reason (1960) reacts against this indiscriminate application of the theoretical principle of freedom.

One of the favorite words of Sartre is *arrachement*. The experience of tearing oneself away from the past, from habit, from a stagnant situation, is dear to him, so dear that, not only the behavior of a fictional character, but a conception of temporality, is based upon it. Twenty years after the publication of *Being and Nothingness* and the first performance of *The Flies*, Sartre wrote in his autobiographical essay, *The Words* :

> I extolled the future at the expense of the present, and the present at the expense of the past. I transformed a quiet evolutionism into a discontinuous and revolutionary catastrophism. A few years ago, I was told that the characters of my plays and novels make their decisions abruptly, that, for instance, Orestes, in *The Flies,* needs only a moment to achieve his conversion. Naturally: it is because I create them in my own image, not as I am, of course, but as I wanted to be. (*Les Mots*, p. 199)

Actually, though the decision of Orestes occurs suddenly, it has nonetheless been prepared. Orestes has expressed his dissatisfaction with his pointless freedom of mind, and, when the decision takes place, he has already dreamed of an act which would involve murder.

"There was nothing left in heaven, neither Good nor Evil." The capitals are somewhat ironical: they stamp values that would be preestablished according to a certain socioreligious code. When Jupiter magically illumines a rock in order to show Orestes that he should not interfere, the latter says: "So that's the Good . . . *Their* Good" (p. 177). Orestes appropriates the word "good" for his personal use: "I accomplished my action, Electra, and this action was good" (p. 208). Of course, by definition, what someone wills is good from his standpoint at the time. But Orestes might say: "I now judge it was wrong." His utterance counts as a decision that the action still appears good to him. Or as a decision to remain faithful to himself? Someone else might speak of stubbornness.

Being and Nothingness identifies experiences of freedom and responsibility. We feel that we decide and have to decide what must be done, what should be best. An experience of freedom so understood may deepen a sense of responsibility, bearing on goals as well as on means. If we accept someone else's judgment, we decide to accept it. On the other hand, a principle of total responsibility may result in paralysis or, as already noted, in levity. I am responsible for everything in any case, so why brood over it? Like *Being and*

Nothingness, Orestes uses the word *angoisse* to name the atmosphere of an awareness of radical responsibility. But, on the whole, his verbal behavior may just as well suggest exhilaration, inebriation with words, juvenile defiance. In such cases, a playwright cannot precisely orient the interpretation of the symptoms, assuming he would like to do so.

Apparently intent on showing he has read *Nausea,* Jupiter speaks of the "obscene and insipid existence" that will be revealed to the Argives (as to Roquentin), if they are deprived of Jupiterian guidelines for proper gestures. Orestes agrees that this revelation throws one into "despair." But the Argives "are free, and human life starts on the other side of despair" (p. 236). *Désespoir* should be understood as the lack of definite hopes, not of the virtue of *espérance* (versus *espoirs*). Lack of religious beliefs does not prevent faith. Activities are experienced as embodying some value, by the very fact that we are active.

The responsibility *Being and Nothingness* talks about is experienced prospectively, not retrospectively. Attempts at self-justification thus appear to be rejected. Echoing *Being and Nothingness,* Orestes asserts he has no excuse and can have no remorse (pp. 235-236). Was it necessary to make Orestes claim that? A spectator might look at the shadow cast by the gesture, and wonder what it is a symptom of.

Jupiter dutifully upholds an authoritarian conception of ethics. He assimilates moral order to natural order: "The world is good; I created it according to my will and I am the Good... This Evil of which you are so proud, whose author you claim to be, is nothing but a reflection of being, an evasion, a misleading image whose very existence is supported by the Good" (pp. 231-232).

In *Being and Nothingness,* human consciousness is characterized as nothingness, lack of nature. So, when Jupiter accuses Orestes of being "unnatural," of having placed himself outside of being, hence of "the Good," he plays conveniently into the hands of Orestes, who retorts: "I shall not return to your nature... For I am a man, Jupiter, and each man must invent his own way" (p. 235). The traditional maxim: "Act according to nature" would become, on the basis of Sartre's ontology: "Act according to the lack of nature." By itself, each formula remains enigmatic: you can play a lot of tricks with the word "nature." If Orestes were a philosopher of science, he might add that natural laws also have to be invented by men, that they are the goals of human activities. Poor Jupiter would then be left with his nothingness. The Sartrean Orestes is more considerate: he lets Jupiter govern stones and stars.

The equation between being and a preestablished Good, nothingness and a preestablished Evil, does not appear in *Being and Nothingness*. In this respect, Jupiter announces the language Sartre will adopt in *Saint Genet* (1952). I have already extracted from *Saint Genet* a note which presents an authentic morality ("impossible today") as a "synthesis of Good and Evil." Apparently, Orestes is not troubled by the impossibility of a synthesis. He is content to say that the idols of Good and Evil have disappeared, and to appropriate the adjective "good" to decorate the fact that he killed Aegisthus and Clytemnestra. Opening "moral perspectives," the end of *Being and Nothingness* simply asks whether it is possible for freedom "to take itself as a value, since it is the source of values" (*L'Etre et le Néant,* p. 722). In my view, looking for this possibility would orient us toward playful activities with no precise preestablished rules. Writing a drama, or an essay, for instance. And this is also what the words of Orestes may suggest to a spectator or reader.

Ostensibily, his goal was to gain citizenship, to root his abstract freedom of mind in his native city. We may think of Sartre getting closer to other Frenchmen during the war years, and turning toward a conception of committed literature.

Orestes fails. Does he even try? His failure does not seem to bother him. He leaves the city without opposition. He generously takes the Furies with him. But, since he said he could not have any remorse, they should be no more than an emblem.

One might say that his goal was to help the Argives come out of their systematic self-hypocrisy, recognize their freedom as the source of values. But his sister, after making a show of rebellion, weakens when Aegisthus and Clytemnestra are killed, and prefers to return to the sin-expiation pattern. Orestes also seems to fail as regards the Argives in general, so that the Furies he takes with him would only be souvenirs from a trip. Does he try to enlighten the Argives, who have not had the privilege of his experience, when he addresses them at the end?

> You can neither punish nor pity me, and this is why I frighten you... Now, I belong with you, my subjects, we are bound by blood, and I deserve to be your king. Your faults and your remorse, your anxiety at night, the crime of Aegisthus, everything is mine, I take everything upon myself. Don't fear your dead any more, they are my dead (p. 224).

After playing Prometheus and Lucifer in the exchange with Jupiter, Orestes plays Christ in front of the Argives. He says a god offered him the throne; he offers himself as a scapegoat instead, but only in effigy. His speech is steeped in mythical fog. Sartre apparently had trouble with the ending.

In the script, a stage direction affixed to the intimidating speech of Jupiter enjoins the actor to adopt a melodramatic, hence ludicrous, tone. No such direction is inserted in the speech of Orestes to the Argives, though he is as grandiloquent as Jupiter.

I have noted Sartre's religiosity in his allegorical uses of the word "Man." In *The Flies,* Orestes takes himself for Man. In *Being and Nothingness,* Sartre chooses a religious label for the type of ethics he is thinking of, and that would presumably transcend self-hypocrisy: "morals of salvation." But the treatise of ethics was not published. Orestes leaves Argos at the end of *The Flies*. Sartre, on the other hand, did not disappear in the wings. He chose to remain stuck on the Parisian stage. And he wrote other plays.

Suppose Orestes had not interfered. Or suppose he had stayed in Argos, without killing Aegisthus and Clytemnestra. Or suppose that, like Electra, he had repented. It could be said, in each case, that he had committed his freedom. For instance, he might have said that he had freely decided to repent.

But these choices would not have put him on a pedestal: alone against everybody else. What seems to matter is his mystical experience, his saying that "freedom swooped down" on him (not on others), his proud defiance. Suppose that Jupiter, in an early attempt to change partners, had enjoined him to kill Aegisthus and Clytemnestra. He would have had not to do that, in order to enjoy a philosophico-dramatic bout with Jupiter. It is with gestures of defiance that a drama can most easily suggest an awareness of ethical freedom.

*   *   *

Orestes has to rely on Jupiter's good will to assert himself and the dignity of Man. Why did the atheistic author of *Being and Nothingness* write a play with a god as one of the characters?

Jupiter cannot be dismissed as a figment of the imagination of the Argives. He exists for Orestes as well as for the others. And he is the most important character structurally. Without him, the play would fly into pieces. He is the only character who can communicate with everyone, who can adapt himself to everyone. Orestes needs him as a fellow-philosopher; he needs him to assert the principle of human autonomy, as only he, Orestes, can present it and assume it. Jupiter may be judged the most enjoyable character in the play;

and, in one sense of this polysemous word, the most "human." Orestes is mostly designed to appeal to more or less young and old people who have acquired or kept youthful aspirations. Drugs, verbal for instance, are not always malefic. It depends on dosage, temperament, circumstances.

Sometimes, Jupiter is reminiscent of a pagan god, sometimes of a Judeo-Christian god, sovereign creator, legislator, judge. But, of course, he is not omniscient: what could be done with an omniscient computer on stage? It would at least preclude characters like Orestes. And Jupiter is far from being omnipotent. He demonstrates a few magic tricks, but he is unaccountably powerless against the decisions of Aegisthus and Orestes.

With them, also with Electra, he cannot be content with short commands. He has to turn to argumentation. His rhetoric succeeds with Electra, who, in *The Flies*, does not enjoy the stature that Giraudoux, more fond of female heroines than Sartre, had granted her in *Electre*. But Jupiter fails against Aegisthus and Orestes.

The character of Jupiter is that of a comedian having some fun, but also lack of fun, playing the role of a god, or the roles of different gods. His magic words ("Abraxas, abraxas, tsé-tsé") are farcical, and he ruins his intimidating speech in the third act by adopting a melodramatic tone. As a god, Jupiter takes himself less seriously than Orestes as a man. In *Being and Nothingness*, the idolatry of ready-made goals, gestures, which serves to mask ethical freedom and responsibility, is called *esprit de sérieux*. But, in *The Flies*, freedom and man, humorlessly extolled by Orestes, become verbal idols themselves.

In *The Words,* Sartre decides he has no superego (*Les Mots,* p. 19). The role of father, during Sartre's childhood, was assumed by a grandfather, whom Sartre pictures as a comedian. Add to this, if you wish, a metamorphosis of Sartre's mother into sister Electra. But, while Sartre makes fun of himself in *The Words,* Orestes, in *The Flies,* is not amused.

The lecture *Existentialism is a Humanism,* published in 1946, contains an apparent contradiction. On the one hand, it is said that "it is quite bothersome that God does not exist, because, with him, the possibility of finding values in an intelligible heaven disappears; there can no longer be an *a priori* good." On the other hand, it is said that, "even if God existed, it would make no difference" (*L'Existentialisme est un humanisme,* pp. 35 and 95).

Actually, Platonists do not need gods to put concepts of values in an intelligible heaven. To me, the first passage means: "It is bothersome for some people." If, on the other hand, one adopts Sartre's viewpoint, the existence of a god theoretically accepted as the proper judge of human activities would make no difference, since you would still have to decide what this god considers it proper for you to do under given circumstances. The situation is different in *The Flies.* Not only does Orestes recognize Jupiter's existence, but Jupiter makes it clear what he wants Orestes to do. However, Orestes does not recognize Jupiter as proper judge.

In *The Words,* after saying he has no superego, Sartre decides that, for him at least, atheism is "a long and cruel task; I think I have pursued it to the end" (*Les Mots*, p. 212). This does not mean that, for a long time, he maintained, like Orestes, the idea of a Platonic Engineer, creator and governor of stars and stones. Nor does it mean that, unlike Orestes, he maintained the idea of a god as proper judge of his activities. To me, it rather means that, like Orestes, he considered himself implicitly to be inhabited by a Holy Ghost called "freedom" and more often "Man." Like everybody else, of course. In *Of Rats and Men,* the allegorical Man is characterized as a tyrant who is supposed to "prey upon" everybody.

(In spiritual matters, I am inclined to consider an indefinite animism as what is least irrational, since a geometric model adapted to brains and other Platonic caves is still not available. I am more in favor of poltergeists than of unique gods and absolute spirits. Sartre's cannibalistic Man is rather "odd" to me, in an Oxford sense. But I am interested in spooks, however christened they may be.)

Being and Nothingness recognizes human incarnation among "things," but it stresses incarnation by the other's glance, and goes so far as to say that only others can set limits to our freedom. What Orestes has to fight is the "objective spirit" of the Argives united in uniform self-hypocrisy. Hamlet, Sartre says, is an individual, but also a myth. Orestes is an individual who has to fight the myth of Father Jupiter with the countermyth of the Holy Ghost (Freedom, Man). By turning the Jupiterian myth into an individual character in the play, Sartre conversely allows an individual character, Orestes, to identify himself with the countermyth.

The clean separation of Jupiter from the Argives makes the task of Orestes easy. He does not have to cope with the Argives individually; and Aegisthus does not resist. Jupiter himself turns into play-acting the obdurate self-hypocrisy of the Argives. One may also see in Jupiter's flippancy a projection of a lack of deep commitment on the part of most Frenchmen toward the current ideology.

The comedian Jupiter does not coincide with the god Jupiter. In their exchange, he provides Orestes with the cues he needs. It is agreed that the god he plays will have power only over stones and stars, and on people to the extent they want to be like stones. Stones are an image that Sartre uses in more than one text to disparage the "spirit of seriousness" (compare Nietzsche's "spirit of heaviness").

There is in Sartre a taste for epic characters. Orestes already shows that; Goetz, in *The Devil and the Good Lord,* much more. But films and narrative fiction are better equipped than dramas to form epic characters; for the activities of such characters have to be quite physical. The principle, laid down in *Being and Nothingness,* that it is others, not things, that limit freedom, fits dramas.

But, in *The Flies,* the Argives do not assume the roles of antagonists who would challenge with countermeanings the meanings Orestes wants to give his gestures, in particular his identification with *the* Holy Ghost. Nor do they fight him physically. They threaten him with all kinds of torture, but are at once subdued by his myth-making speech (because it is Greek to them?). This is the main factor of disanalogy between Orestes and Resistance fighters. Having got rid of a compliant Jupiter, Orestes delivers his stunning speech and flees without opposition, leaving innocuous "stones" behind.

*   *   *

At the end of this section, I had better spell out my own position concerning such words as "freedom" and "determination."

Experiences are lived in atmospheres of freedom and constraint, to various extents. So, "freedom" and "constraint" could name the poles of a concept. To speak of illusion in this perspective, to say that someone "believes" he is free, but is not "really" free, would be inapposite. What is experienced is basic, what is thought about someone is not.

Signs are what is experienced. Signifying is experienced. What signifies determines what is signified. This determination is projected on the plane of what is signified. The signified elements appear to cohere more or less, thus to determine (signify) one another.

There are various types of meaning, hence of coherence. Conceptual (philosophical) consistency, mathematical necessity, poetic consonance, are not temporal. Temporal coherences (determinations) are of two types:

causality and destiny.

Causality is the limit of probability. Causally, events determine one another under their general (recurrent) aspect: whenever an event of type X occurs, it is followed by an event of type Y.

Destiny determines events under their singular aspect. The postulate that the historical field is one is the postulate that each singular event signals and is signalled by all other events, past and future: predestination and postdestination are equivalent. But I am not a divine computer. I determine (decide) some future and past events, and then change these determinations, in the midst of ignorance and in atmospheres of varying certainty and uncertainty. I appeal to causal proverbs for partial help. Causality is a lack of destiny.

Instead of that, fictional processes may be composed. They are more manageable. A playful activity leaves future events fairly undetermined. But a ludic atmosphere makes the uncertainty of the future pleasant. Esthetic contemplation gets rid of uncertainty. If the esthetic world is felt to be well composed, and if it is of a temporal type (fiction), experiences of freedom and destiny may coincide. I identify with the determination (destination) of a coherent (destined) world. This is how I would interpret the classical equation of freedom with necessity. I view it as an example of estheticism, or religiosity, already suggested by the esthetic meaning of *mundus* and *cosmos*. Some theoretical decorators have applied cosmetics to the historical field, with its oceans of ignorance and chasms of pain, so that it may pass for a well composed novel or drama to be contemplated at leisure.

Sartre relies on experiences of freedom. But he reduces them to the experience of deciding; and he even stresses the experience of having to decide, which tends to subordinate freedom to constraint. Furthermore, he remains under the spell of *être* (to be); he gives it precedence over *éprouver* (to feel, experience). To get rid of the bothersome variety of experiences, he speaks of "human reality" in the singular. Man is free, is freedom, is condemned to be free. Thus we return to traditional quarrels over the freedom of an allegorical figure nicknamed Man, or God.

NO EXIT (1944)

Garcin is introduced into a drawing-room, with no mirror and no windows. According to the usher, or bell-boy, one does not sleep in this place, and there is no "outside." Two women, Inès and Estelle, arrive, and it appears gradually that the three characters are "dead" and that they are in "Hell." They realize that they have been put into one room in order to torment one another with words. Inès is a lesbian who tries to seduce Estelle, an infanticide, who tries to seduce Garcin. Not only does the presence of Inès bother Garcin, but he insists on being judged by her and he wants to persuade her that he was not a coward. Estelle attempts to kill Inès with a paper knife, forgetting that they are already "dead." The three characters appear to realize that they are condemned to remain together forever, and to continue as they have started.

*   *   *

Hells and Heavens are legendary. On the one hand, they are not part of the historical field. They are transcendent; they are detached like an esthetic world. On the other hand, this is *where we* are supposed to go *after* death. If there are spatial and temporal relations between them and the Earth, they are part of the historical field.

Requirements of coherence can intervene once a type of signification, hence logic, has been adopted. But relations between what signifies and what is signified remain transcendent. For instance, if historical signification is used to subordinate the others, it may be said that, in the case of a theatrical performance, experienced signs signify historical actors (and spectators), who signify ludic actors (and spectators), who signify esthetic characters. At this point, the direction may be inverted. Characters may be interpreted as signifying ludic and historical individuals. In a vaguer way, of course: "significance" disperses. It is disorderly, entropic. These uses of "to signify" bridge absolute gaps between types of entities.

No Exit makes a clever use of the transcendent aspect of Hells to isolate a fictional field. The historical aspect of Hells is subdued, since it is unlikely that spectators will take seriously this fictional Hell as a picture of the kind of afterlife they will have to go through.

The characters of *No Exit* have remembrances of their past lives and visions of what is happening on "Earth," while they are quarrelling. This would be legend within the fiction. However, time in the fictional Hell is distinguished at one point from time on the fictional Earth. Garcin says that his wife "died a moment ago" (Hell time); and he adds: "About two months ago" (Earth time). Above all, the conditions of existence in the fictional Hell are shown to be radically different.

The medieval idea of Hell is endless physical tortures. To the characters' surprise, the Hell of *No Exit* avoids that. It is more reminiscent of a pagan conception that reduces the dead to shades. In the *Odyssey*, Ulysses attracts a flock of shades with the smell of blood. What they miss is the full embodiment of carnivorous animals.

The shades of *No Exit* are not blood-thirsty. One might say they are glance-thirsty. They have trouble adjusting to the fact that they are reduced to pure gesturing. There is a strong reflexive aspect in *No Exit*. By this I mean that the characters appear as comedians, as being only capable of playing the roles of characters. Being dead means, in this case, that the utilitarian frame, the historical background of ludic activities, has been taken away.

So the characters cannot be tortured physically. They cannot kill one another, as Estelle realizes: the paper knife is only a prop. In their ludic roles, actors cannot kill one another. The setting of *No Exit* is a drawing-room, not a dungeon, not a torture chamber. In a drawing-room, you are, or were, supposed only to talk, and to talk as if you were on stage. The temporality of a ludic role is detached from utilitarian temporality. An "eternal" present tense (which I called a metatense) may be used to talk about ludic roles or esthetic characters: "Sartre says," "Garcin says." If playing a part is not improvised, what the actors say is determined by the text; to some extent, an acting style is imposed by a director. In *No Exit,* Garcin expresses the opinion the trio is manipulated, that everything has been foreseen. On the whole, however, the characters of *No Exit* play-act as if they were improvising. Finally, the last words in *No Exit* : "Let's continue" may give a spectator the impression that the three characters will hardly be able to innovate. The analogy, in this case, would be with several performances of one dramatic script, with some variants.

*   *   *

The connections between *No Exit* and *Being and Nothingness* are not as obtrusive as in *The Flies*: there is no philosophico-dramatic bout between two characters. But overlaps are as extensive. *The Flies* emphasizes freedom as decision and invention, at least in the character of Orestes: everybody has to, and can, "invent his way." *No Exit* absorbs the properly metadramatic aspect of *Being and Nothingness* pretty thoroughly. What need do we have of a god? We are judged by others. To this extent, they incarnate us, objectify us, and limit our freedom.

In Plato, the human cave is the body, the skull, the senses. According to the Sartre of *Being and Nothingness*, it is the other's glance that reminds us of our unjustified existence, and may frustrate our goals, in particular if the goal is to justify what we already have done. If Sartre chooses glances as a synecdoche for judging, it is probably because eyes are the most spiritual feature of human bodies. But some nonhuman animals have eyes; and some people are blind.

The human cave sketched in *Being and Nothingness* is mostly a theatrical stage, with antagonistic gesturing. Cannot one ignore, or escape, the "tyranny of the human face," the "primitive sorcery" that Sartre attributes to eyes in *Visages* (*Les Ecrits de Sartre*, p. 564)? An opportunity is offered to Garcin in *No Exit* : the door opens, he can flee offstage. But he decides to stay, not because of the coquettish and irritating Estelle, but of the antagonistic Inès. Perversely, he insists on being judged by her; he wants to persuade her that he was not a coward on "Earth," which is what matters to him:

> It is you I must convince; we belong to the same race. Did you think I was going to leave? I could not leave you here, triumphant, with all these thoughts in your head, all these thoughts that concern me . . . She does not count. But you, who hate me, if you believe me, I shall be saved (pp. 87-88).

If he fled, he would still have the impression of being seen. Etymologically, ideas are what is to be seen. Platonic Ideas are objects of contemplation. "Visual" judgments, in *No Exit*, are not esthetic contemplations.

I have suggested that *No Exit* offers to the characters a pure ludic field, since death reduces them to gesturing. But they have trouble adjusting. They do not develop an amusing lovers' quarrel, or a farcical exchange of Rabelaisian insults, for instance.

In *No Exit*, Estelle thinks it is nicer to say that she and the other two are "absent," rather than "dead." This euphemism is taken from common French parlance. Mallarmé and Genet link esthetic or ludic existence with death and absence (detachment, purification). Genet's characters aim at a ludic and esthetic purification (there remains some religious coating). So, "death" receives a favorable connotation. Sartre, on the other hand, is loath to separate, even in theory, historical from fictional existence, ludic activities and esthetic contemplation from utilitarian activities and values.

For instance, in *Critique of Dialectical Reason*, he insists that his philosophizing has cognitive value. He wants to prove, to show necessity. But philosophy can only play with words against words. Words are neither mathematical symbols nor experimental instruments. All that a philosopher can do is drug himself with words like "necessity," "demonstrate," "the truth." The allegorical reader that Sartre sets out to convince may be reduced to the Sartre-Roquentin who emphasizes gratuitousness, a basic lack of justification.

Genet's characters would enjoy the conditions that *No Exit* provides. Sartre's characters do not, *in part* because they still retain an earth-like outlook, which confuses utilitarian and ludic perspectives.

Garcin's slogan "Hell is the others" (p. 92) has relevance to conditions on Earth to the extent that we accept the stress which *Being and Nothingness* lays on antagonism in human relations. But, at least, there are some avenues of escape. We can sleep, dream. This is denied to the characters in *No Exit.* If we insist on being judged, we can invent the Other (a compliant god, conscience, posterity). The three characters are deprived of mirrors. We can work and play with things. In the setting of *No Exit,* there is only an unmanageable bronze statue, the emblem of a frozen past.

Being and Nothingness considers the future as open. We may try to change the judgments of others, which bear on our past and present, with decisions, plans, that project us toward the future. Of course, we shall die. But death is a receding horizon, except in cases such as that of people condemned to die at a definite time in the immediate future (see Sartre's short story, *The Wall*). In *No Exit,* the characters are already "dead." And they seem unable to distinguish between a ludic future, that might be open, and a utilitarian future, which is what is dead.

Even from a ludic standpoint, it must be confessed that they are not offered a promising situation. Playing the harp, contemplating a divine computer, or even attending philosophical colloquia in the Elysean fields with participants that more than pretend to understand one another and themselves, are not visions of bliss for me. In *No Exit,* the characters are restricted to talking games with two partners-opponents in a cramped space. And they are well-assorted only from a devilish, or impish, standpoint. Each character wants to play his own game, and use as partner-opponent the one that does not fit.

Estelle wants to play love with Garcin, who at first refuses. Since he is only interested in being assured he was not a coward, she agrees readily. Too readily: he wants to win over a tougher opponent. Inès offers the devoted mirror of her eyes to Estelle, who prefers to win over Garcin. The latter finally complies, adding caressing hands and embracing arms to eyes, but he is bothered by the presence of Inès, who does not fail to call him a coward.

The characters, especially Garcin, still want to win instead of playing well. If winning is everything, or the main thing, play cannot be detached from utilitarian work. In his theory of *littérature engagée*, or in the style he sometimes adopts, especially in *Critique*, Sartre writes as if the objective of literary and philosophical games was to win.

In *No Exit*, the conditions are such that, even if the characters purified their perspective, their kind of Hell (there are worse kinds) would not be turned into a kind of Heaven. But it could at least become a Purgatory. Toward the end, the three characters burst into laughter. This gesture may be interpreted as a purification of their perspective, as the start of a play in the spirit of Genet (I am thinking of the recommendations of stage director Archibald in *Les Nègres*). But Sartre prefers to bring *No Exit* to a close.

*　　*　　*

Garcin is interested in justifying his life on Earth in the eyes of Inès. Not his whole life: he is interested only in proving to Inès that he was not a coward. He can no longer do anything on Earth that would tend to modify the judgments of others: "I left my life in their hands . . . Before, I could act . . . I have become public property" (p. 81). He can only play-act as his own defender, enlisting Inès to play-act as proper judge. This can continue indefinitely. New arguments, new rhetorical devices can be resorted to. There are no mathematical rules to this game; there is no divine computer to apply them. If Inès agrees, this will not prove that Garcin was not a coward. It will simply prove that he was a clever defender, that he has won as an orator. Neither on Earth nor in this kind of afterlife can there be a Last Judgment.

Like some games, a society has laws. And there are also unofficial rules of etiquette. Social rules inextricably mix playful and moral goals and values. Setting up a god as proper referee, apart from social rules and rulers, may be viewed as a half-hearted attempt to turn a moral into a ludic perspective. From the standpoint of a transcendent god, we should be fictional individuals, merely players. From his standpoint, we should not have to win, to be successful in our moral efforts, in preventing or alleviating some suffering. We should only have to play and have played well. The role of the Villain for instance.

Estelle and Inès are not interested in redeeming their past lives, in winning a favorable judgment from people on Earth or from their two companions. They are interested in the present, more precisely in a love game. But the atmosphere lacks playfulness.

Being and Nothingness analyzes love in a way that may be contrasted with Plato's in the *Phaedrus,* and with the poetico-religious tradition that stems from it, a tradition which turns words of love into love of words, as Apollinaire points out in *Rosemonde* : "I nicknamed her Rosemonde" (*Alcools,* p. 104). *Being and Nothingness* presents love as a project to seduce (and be seduced), to be justified in the eyes of the person to be won over: I shall justify your existence so that you can justify mine.

Love is an attempt to form a utilitarian alliance as well as a playful partnership. But, to remain active, the perspective must also cast the other person in the role of antagonist. The trouble, from my standpoint, is that an erotic perspective so sketched does not distinguish between utilitarian and playful antagonist. An enemy should be avoided or killed. Not an opponent. Concerning love and other matters, *Being and Nothingness* does not stress this distinction. Neither do Estelle and Inès in *No Exit.* Unlike Garcin, they have abandoned their utilitarian past: no regret, no remorse (like Orestes). But, in the present, they have not yet realized that their incarnation can only be ludic: pure theatrical gestures. Inès is jealous; Estelle attempts to kill her.

An opponent must also be your partner in some way: otherwise no game. So one might speak of a ludic synthesis. But this word had better be left to chemists, and the word "infinite" to mathematicians. In an essay about a text or set of texts, a suitable partner-opponent can be composed without having to deal with a referee (there are no preestablished rules), and without striving to win against a utilitarian enemy (though a few critics still write as if they had to prove something and convince an allegorical reader). I compose my Sartre. Someone else will compose his, if he wishes. There need be no jealousy. The utilitarian Sartre is past caring, supposing he ever did: he had other fish to fry.

Being and Nothingness considers love as sexual. This fits the general strategy: show that we have to incarnate each other, instead of just embodying ourselves in relations with things. Love is a project to justify flesh in an uneasily passive-active atmosphere, as opposed to more definitely ludic sports.

Do some people manage to turn love-making into a candidly spectacular sport, in spite of the poor resources that human bodies offer to this kind of exercise? All I can say is that I am not much of a voyeur. Some wrestling bouts are farces, but less uncouth than pornographic films. If they are serious, they may be appreciated like the performances of acrobats, rather than clowns.

Anyhow, while not esthetically proper in terms of, say, Racinian requirements, the Estelle-Garcin scrum does not turn into a pornographic episode. Inès sees that it does not. Still, I am bothered by such things as Garcin's words to Estelle when, at first, he refuses to play: "You are an octopus, you are a swamp" (p. 84); or his wish that a medieval Hell be substituted for his Sartrean Hell, physical torture for psychological exasperation. I know; such outbursts may be received as hyperboles that Sartre lends some of his characters to contribute to their delineation. Still, such words, while they may indicate the trouble the characters experience in adjusting their language to the situation, also jar with the basic postulate of the play. Mortal flesh, which can be tortured and sexually desirable or disgusting, is gone.

In a way, *No Exit* may be said to arrange a *situation limite*. But the exceptionality of the situation consists in a reduction of existence to pure gestures, not in a confrontation with death as one branch of an alternative. What is exceptional is that the characters cannot kill themselves or one another. Furthermore, in this short one-act play, which is fairly static, though suspense and variations are adroitly managed, no character makes a decision that would change the situation, allow him to find a way out. Unlike Orestes, Garcin refuses to disappear offstage.

Each character appears as a *caractère* : Garcin is someone who is interested only in being judged not to be a coward; the lesbian Inès and the frivolous Estelle are interested only in two versions of erotic seduction. The play does not allow, for instance, Garcin to play the role of Inès, Inès that of Estelle, Estelle that of Garcin (contrast Genet's *Les Bonnes*). The male-female distribution of set personalities may strike one as a cliché. The play could have exposed this stereotype. Instead of that, it relies upon its acceptance by spectators or readers.

*   *   *

In my opinion, it is very unlikely that a spectator, or reader, should infer that the playwright took seriously his version of an afterlife. Unlikely, but not impossible. Students and fellow-critics have taught me that, in matters of interpretation, especially concerning significance, nothing is impossible. It may well be that some spectators, or readers, decided that they had better not be infanticides, lesbians, or cowards (and forgot about it at once). More plausibly, a maxim such as "Live by yourself" may be drawn from the aphorism "Hell is the others."

As far as I know and can remember, Sartre has always remained negative, or agnostic, on the subject of an afterlife. In *The Words,* he formulates the vague notion of a survival of humans among humans, in an Auguste Comte fashion. Not according to the French criteria of glory. There may already have sprung up, while I am writing this, a *rue,* or *théâtre,* or *square* Jean-Paul-Sartre, perhaps even an *avenue,* if avenues are not reserved for Charles-de-Gaulle and Albert-Camus. But this is not what he meant. He meant an insidious, anonymous "haunting" of what humans would be thinking. For better or for worse; he would not have relished innocuousness. There is a similar dream in *Orlando,* by Virginia Woolf. But the hero-heroine is thinking of plants, not humans. I see in this contrast a symptom of a divergence between poetic and dramatic aspirations. I feel closer to Woolf, of course. She would make a poor opponent. Sartre is not insensitive to nonhuman elements. But his sensibility to these elements, which shows in his novels more than in his plays, has a narrow range; and it often appears uneasy. Sartre stopped publishing narrative fiction in 1949, dramatic fiction ten years later.

Sartre's theory of committed literature was written a few years after *No Exit.* Yet this drama is remarkably devoid of any particular relevance to a contemporary situation. This may be one of the reasons why it has not aged much in my judgment. The opprobrium attached to lesbianism may have faded; but, in any case, if it is mentioned in the play, it does not have any impact on the plot. I have noted what I take to be faults. But nothing is perfect; and I still consider *No Exit* as Sartre's best play. This opinion seems to be shared by quite a few people, for instance by Robert Lorris in his *Sartre Dramaturge.* Such agreements should not be taken as either good or bad things.

DEAD WITHOUT BURIAL (1946)

Dead without Burial (*Morts sans Sépulture,* once translated as *The Victors*) takes place (legendarily) in the French Alps toward the end of the second world war. The characters are divided into two groups: Resistance fighters (Sorbier, Canoris, Henri, Lucie, and her fifteen-year old brother, François), and members of the Vichy militia (Clochet, Pellerin, Landrieu), who have captured them and attempt to extract information about their leader by torture. The latter, Jean, who was on his way to warn other members of the Resistance of an ambush, is captured in his turn and locked in with his companions. But his false identity holds. So the others now have something to conceal. Sorbier manages to kill himself, Henri strangles François, who threatened to talk. Jean is released. Lucie, Canoris, and Henri finally decide to give false, but plausible, information in exchange for their lives. But Clochet has them shot.

*   *   *

The setting is cleverly chosen and well integrated. It is a rural school-house and the scenes oscillate between an attic where the prisoners are kept and a classroom downstairs where they are brought one by one in order to be interrogated. Upstairs, the prisoners are surrounded with discarded junk; and the classroom is used for an unexpected kind of questioning. There are both a similarity and an opposition between the normal use of the two rooms and what is made of them in the play.

Upstairs, the outside world is represented by a human character: Jean. Downstairs, it is represented by a radio set which delivers news about war operations from the English and German sides, and coded messages (the landing in Normandy has just taken place). The set also provides music, in opposition to screams of pain and, at the end, to the sounds of shots which signal the execution of Lucie, Canoris, and Henri. Also to be noted: it is the intervention of a nonhuman element, a rainfall, which softens Lucie's attitude. It is at this point that she agrees with Canoris that they should swallow their pride and give false information, in order to survive.

*   *   *

Dead without Burial is Sartre's play in which a dialectic between individuals and groups is best developed. To some extent, each character is motivated by a we-they opposition, except for the young François (this exception adds to the spectrum). Each character wants to show his allegiance, and contribute to the victory of his group. But the Vichy men are haunted by the certainty that the war is lost. Whether they succeed in forcing the prisoners to talk or not does not matter in this respect. All that Landrieu can say is: "It looks bad when they don't talk" (p. 140). In the other camp, the idea that the Allies are winning is no great comfort. Until Jean is brought in, they have nothing to say that would be useful to the torturers. The two teams are isolated, closer to each other than to their outside allies, and to their collective cause. The utilitarian perspective is thus reduced. As in *No Exit,* the characters seem to be limited to pure gestures. But, as far as the prisoners are concerned, the hell they are in is much more medieval than the hell of *No Exit.* The reduction of usefulness does not produce a reduction of nastiness on the part of the Vichy men. It was during the last days of the war that some of the losers were at their worst. They wanted to get revenge for losing.

Within each team, Sartre has skillfully arranged differences and conflicts. Unlike Landrieu, Clochet enjoys torturing for the sake of torturing. To some extent, he has to turn the enemy into an ally. He has to empathize with the victim, without being tortured himself of course. A ludic empathy? Religious rather. It is the kind of empathy which, to my mind, makes Aristotelian catharsis a very dubious justification of tragic sublimation. In *Le Théâtre et Après,* Jean Duvignaud adopts the interpretation of tragic characters as scapegoats offered to the delectation of a community. I do not deny the socioreligious origin of the theatre. I do not deny that some plays may offer to spectators an opportunity to be sadistic voyeurs on a collective or individual basis. Burning, quartering, hanging used to be popular festivals. But whether it should be the goal of playwrights to offer fac-similes of this kind of festival is another question.

Sorbier tells Clochet: "We are brothers. I attract you, don't I? It is not I that you torture. It is yourself" (p. 154). This gesture may be interpreted as an attempt to counterattack with words, only words. While Henri is being tortured, Clochet speaks to him in an empathetic way which repels Landrieu. The latter is interested in torture only as a utilitarian activity. The means have to conform to the goals.

In the Resistance team, a rift occurs between Jean, the leader, who has not been identified and is going to be released, and the others. Jean was Lucie's lover. But, when she is brought back after being tortured and raped, she says that she is beyond love, that she does not feel (does not want to feel?) anything any longer. Henri excludes Jean from the team, when he says the purpose is to win, that is to say, not to talk. The young François is not interested in winning; he wants to be protected by his sister, who lets him be strangled by Henri. Jean accuses Henri of having acted out of pride. Canoris is presented as a pragmatic militant who is concerned only with usefulness. At the beginning, he says: "We have been dead for a long time: since the moment we stopped being useful" (p. 110). Toward the end, it is he who tries to persuade Lucie and Henri to give false information about Jean, so that they may be allowed to survive and perhaps be useful again: "If you let yourself be killed when you can still work, there will be nothing more absurd than your death" (p. 211). However, Sartre was in his most tragic mood. Clochet has the trio shot. Offstage, so we are not told what Canoris thought then.

Henri says: "I was given orders. I obeyed. I felt justified. Now nobody can give me orders and nothing can justify me any longer" (p. 110). To some extent, he echoes Orestes. But he does not enjoy the fact that he can no longer hide his freedom of choice in blind obedience, in functioning like a machine. Of course, his situation is quite different from that of Orestes, who had only a compliant god to contend with, and who had the impression that he could do something.

An echo of *Being and Nothingness* may also be discerned in these words of Henri: "I am not missing anywhere, I did not leave any hole . . . I slipped off the world and it has remained full. Like an egg" (p. 113). Goals give a dynamic existence to consciousness, which is defined as nothingness, lack of being. Without goals, it reduces to a stagnant shadow of the world. Sorbier views Jean's arrival as a piece of bad luck. Henri, on the contrary, welcomes the purpose it provides: now, he has something to conceal.

                              *   *   *

In *Dead without Burial,* Sartre has attempted to bring repeated evocations of torture into an esthetic world. Torture most often takes place offstage (but screams are heard). In two cases (Henri's and Sorbier's), it takes place on stage. It is also on stage that Henri strangles François.

A passage of *What is Literature?* evokes the Occupation years in Paris, when systematic torturing was known or surmised to take place around the corner. The passage sees in torturing an absolute evil which denies Leibnizian whitewashing. It also pictures the torturer-tortured relation in sexual terms. At the end, Sartre defines torturing as a "mass in which two freedoms have communed in the destruction of what is human" (*Situations,* II, p. 248). The adoption of a black mass label is hardly a way to get rid of a religious mentality. A substitution of "Man" for "God" cannot even pass for a proposal of a new countermyth.

(Perhaps it should be recalled that, in this essay, "religious" and "religiosity" apply to confusions between meanings, values, of which myths (legends and allegories) are symptoms, if they are not recognized as myths. In some cases, religiosity may help someone without being harmful to others. Mystiques come under the head of religiosity. Mystical experiences do not. But someone called a mystic may resort to myth, instead of turning toward pure poetry. A pure poem attempts to create a limited mystical experience with words and in spite of words. Poetry has to break prose arrangements, in particular legendary and allegorical figures. I adopt the conception of poetry presented in *What is Literature?*. But without the derogatory ingredients.)

I do consider overwhelming pain as the worst moral antivalue. But, from my standpoint, it hardly matters what or who inflicts pain on what or whom. When political conditions do not allow them safely to display their skills on anthropomorphic animals, biological inquisitors can claim to be celebrating white masses for the greater glory of our Lord Man. Furthermore, human witches are not needed to experience grave pain. In English, as opposed to French, there is a choice between "human" and "humane." Yet, "inhuman" is often used to brand behaviors that appear to be special to humans.

If some anthropomorphic animal, while being tortured, can spiritualize the antisense of his experience by seeing it as a black mass which desecrates the carrot of Man (or God), good for him. Any kind of effective tactic should be applauded under such circumstances. But what about the victims, human or not, of atrocious pain, inflicted by humans or not, who cannot make an effective use of this anesthetic? (The trouble is not only a powerlessness of a victim or would-be helper; it is also cognitive uncertainty: how do I know what someone or something feels? How do I know how I would or shall feel? Symptoms and memories are all that can be observed.)

I appreciate the fact that Sartre has a broader range as novelist and dramatist than as a theorist. There are sexual overtones in *Dead without Burial*; but at least the characters do not talk about black masses. The question is: how can evocations of grave physical pain be esthetically converted in a play to be performed, if at all?

Some scandalized or disgusted spectators protested or left during the first performance of *Dead without Burial*. Sartre says: "Thanks to them, I discovered, and, I must confess, I was stupefied, the true merit of classical discretion: you must not show everything" (*Un Théâtre de Situations*, p. 94). Both Plato and Aristotle choose wonder as the trigger of philosoophical reflection. I doubt that the stupefaction alleged by Sartre can pass for philosophical wonder. Everyone has his blind spots. If you choose to concentrate on something, you choose to forget the rest. But I sometimes find Sartre's shows of naiveté and credulity (in political matters, especially) hardly credible. In this particular case, I prefer to think that he attempted an experiment.

Screaming and writhing are more impressive symptoms than conventional verbal gestures, which vary with tongues. To exclaim *Ouye,* or, more decorously, *Aïe* (not "Ouch"), is to play the part of a Francophone in pain.

Even screaming may be conventional. On the average, women are still supposed, I think, to scream more than men. This does not mean that they are less courageous; on the average again, it seems that, if less brave, they are more courageous; they have to. It may simply mean that they are better equipped to relieve a pressure, or, more plausibly, that conventions allow them more easily to channel a disturbance into this kind of gesturing. Such play-acting may be irritating or funny. In *Dead without Burial,* Clochet says of Henri that "he screamed like a woman" (p. 204). But Lucie does not scream. In any case, screaming, under the circumstances, could hardly pass for a conventional gesture.

Farcical caricatures allow spectators not to be disturbed by an impression that interjections or screams are symptoms of pain. A comic character is the character of a comedian. Screaming caricaturally, a comic character (an actor) shows that he is not flogged, but reacts properly to a gesture of flogging. Are tragic characters allowed to appear as characters of tragedians? Comedy can go deeper than tragedy in that it can expose tragic characters as comedians.

It appears to me there is a lack of ludic and esthetic integrity, an imposture, an incompatibility, in an attempt to create dramatic ghosts and at the same time to suggest they are not ghosts. One might speak of a pathetic fallacy. The term has been applied to lyrical poems to the extent that they personify, thus are dramatic (whether what is personified is anthropomorphic or not matters little in fiction). Symptoms of anxiety are all right, but not symptoms of grave physical pain.

A criticism of tragedies such as that of Plato could orient the outlook toward moral questions. Does a theatrical exploitation of symptoms of grave physical pain train people to be content to enjoy ineffectual compassion under all circumstances? Does it encourage cruelty? I suspect the repercussions are diverse, or negligible. So I limit myself to meta-esthetic considerations.

I do not mean that grave physical pain should be banned as a topic. Obviously, it should not be banned in moral exhortations or in metamoral discourse. I mean that evocations such as those that occur in *Dead without Burial* do not fit a dramatic show. Their gestural meaning is too weak to take care of the symptomatic meaning. If a spectator experiences the gestural meaning as strong enough, the evocations of torture are turned into jokes. Sartre said that, during rehearsals, an actor was eating a sandwich while uttering screams. The performances were not supposed to offer the spectators such a comic conversion.

*　　*　　*

In his own comments on this play, Sartre contrasts its historical setting, close to the present, with that of *The Flies* : "Today, I would not write a play like *The Flies*" (*Un Théâtre de Situations*, p. 241). Yet, a few years later, he situated *The Devil and the Good Lord* in the sixteenth century. Besides, in 1946, the state of affairs which serves as a background in *Dead without Burial* had already ceased to exist. So the spectators could consider that the topic was no longer relevant. Of course, as far as the evocation of torture is concerned, the play never lost is relevance. Far from it.

Dead without Burial definitely pictures an extreme situation. The situation narrows the range of choices, but does not eliminate possibilities. Rather, it sharpens the awareness of having to decide, even if the characters can choose only ineffectual gestures. Suicide is a possibility that remains. This is what Sorbier chooses. The others see their alternative as talking versus not talking. One might even say: screaming versus not screaming. But this would be going too far: they simply wonder whether they will scream.

For someone who relishes a tight dialectic between individuals, complicated by relations between individuals and groups, *Dead without Burial* should be Sartre's most impressive drama. One might say his most powerful drama. But its power may easily backfire. For it relies on the acceptance of direct and renewed evocations of torture as esthetic fuel.

THE RESPECTFUL PROSTITUTE (1946)

The setting of *The Respectful Prostitute* is the apartment of Lizzie. A negro, who has been falsely accused of raping Lizzie and has so far managed to escape, beseeches her to tell the truth to the judge. She promises to do so, in order to get rid of him. She has spent the night with Fred, the son of a senator. Fred wants her to accuse the negro, so as to disculpate a cousin of his who has killed a companion of the black man. Fred fails, but, with clever words about a grieving mother, his father manages to make Lizzie sign a false statement. Later, the black man, who is pursued by a lynching mob, reappears. Lizzie hides him. But Fred comes back. The black man runs away. After a show of rebellion, Lizzie accepts Fred's offer to keep her in style for his own personal use.

*　　*　　*

Except for the amateurish *Bariona, The Respectful Prostitute,* which was hastily written to complement *Dead without Burial* on the same program, is Sartre's poorest play.

According to *What is Literature?,* a drama should deal with issues that are of direct concern to the audience for whom it is intended. Sartre's plays are written for a French, not a Usonian, audience (I say "Usonian" to avoid the ambiguity of "American"). No doubt, racism is a universal phenomenon. For instance, I prefer quadrupeds to centipedes; among quadrupeds, Persians to Siamese. But the ways in which racism is alluded to in the play were not French. Actually, there were very few blacks in metropolitan France at the time. It would have been more suitable to choose as a legendary setting a country which was still a French colony.

I suspect that most French spectators were incited to reflect that this type of racism was not French, not that racism was also a French phenomenon. Sartre may have banked on an irritation with Usonia derived from the conviction that, without Usonian troops, France would not have been liberated. Add to this feeling of inferiority the fact, or rumor, that, for a few months, some sacred Parisian bread was made of corn ordered from Usonia instead of wheat, because the king's English was considered the only honorable kind. And, for most Parisians, maize, I mean corn, was for pigs, I mean hogs.

If Sartre's theory is adopted, the task of portraying Usonian realities and unrealities should be left to Usonian writers. Sartre had stayed a short time in the States, and had written a few impressions. He had not stayed long enough for a French writer to tell his compatriots all about Usonia. That took a few more weeks.

One detail is worth a note. Fred, who, otherwise, is fond of talking about sin and the devil, says that his cousin is "a leader, which is all that counts" (p. 38), and that he himself has "the right to live," that he is "expected" (p. 82). This is the kind of language that Lucien, in the novelette *L'Enfance d'un Chef* (*Childhood of a Leader*), included in *Le Mur,* had already adopted, as he tried to justify his existence in his own eyes and escape a feeling of gratuitousness.

In *Nausea* (1938), Roquentin reaches a fundamental revelation of superfluity, of a lack of *raison d'être.* The webs of causes and functions are dissolved. In *The Words* (1964), Sartre portrays himself as having been imbued very early with the impression he had a mission, that he was called upon (by whom, or what?) to write, and, at the same time, as being struck with the gratuitousness of existence: "The abstract postulation of my necessity and the raw intuition of my existence subsist side by side without fighting or mingling" (*Les Mots,* p. 206). So, after all, everything cannot be reduced to contradictions, dramatic conflicts, and attempts at syntheses all the time. I assume that an impression of being necessary, of having received a mandate, remains as a stubborn faith in oneself, and that it is a necessary, though insufficient, condition, for enjoying, or being afflicted with, as brilliant a career as that of Jean-Paul Sartre or Charles de Gaulle. But Sartre remained troopless.

At the end of *Nausea,* Roquentin decides that writing a novel will deliver him from his aimlessness, and "save" him, "in the past, only in the past." This ending is reminiscent of *Le Temps Retrouvé* in which Proust speaks of what literature should be. Proust apparently attempts to persuade himself that the book the character pronamed "I" decides to write is precisely the one that ends with *LeTemps Retrouvé*, though it is said, self-contradictorily, that a literary text should not contain metaliterary theory. In the case of *Nausea, Nausea* does not seem to be the sort of book Roquentin had in mind. Still, it afforded Sartre the opportunity to write (according to his mandate, to necessity) a book about the gratuitousness of existence.

The Respectful Prostitute does not present Fred and his notion of the leader in a favorable light. At the end of *Childhood of a Leader,* Lucien's decision to become a leader (the boss of his father's small factory), and the mythical vision of his life, justified by the flock of workers he will lead, are presented sarcastically.

At the end of *Nausea,* Roquentin is not thinking of workers, but readers. Thinking about prospective readers allows him to dream of a "salvation." In *What is Literature?*, Sartre decides that *the* writer attempts to feel essential in relation to *the* world, thanks to *the* reader. But there are diverse readers, if any, let alone diverse writers. The readers should be united into one audience, an audience that would turn the countermyth it absorbs into practical action: an army, a team of workers.

I return to my refrain: ludic activities are not distinguished from moral activities. Sometimes, moral and playful goals are compatible; most often, they are not. Moral activities have to be imperialistic: it is in the historical field, assumed to be one, that I have to fight evils; and I must try to enlist others in tasks that I judge to be benefic, whatever their opinion may be. If writing is a ludic activity, it is not oriented in the same way as straight propaganda or information.

Essays may define what counts as moral goals. These metamoral definitions may be viewed as moral commitments. But, if I write an essay, it is because I am not satisfied with some definitions or lacks of definition. I claim the right to define. Accordingly, I recognize the same right to others, indeed encourage them to exert this right. Rhetorically, this is not a good tactic. On the basis of their temperaments and backgrounds, it is probable that others will want to slice the conceptual cake differently. Unless they are not interested in playing this verbal game at all. At least, an essay can make its metamoral axioms pretty clear. A poem or a piece of fiction cannot.

DIRTY HANDS (1948)

The play takes place in "Illyria," which is supposed to stand for an East European country, toward the end of the second world war. Hugo, just out of prison, arrives at the house of a friend and fellow-communist, Olga. Hugo had been ordered to kill Hoederer, the secretary of the Party, because of his policy of collaboration with bourgeois organizations. Now, the Party line has changed: Hoederer's policy has been approved by the Russians. Hugo has become a thorn. Olga obtains a few hours of respite from those who have come to get rid of Hugo. She wants to see if he can serve again, and she asks him to recount the whole story.

Instead of being told, Hugo's story is dramatized, and it takes up the major portion of the play. Hugo had been placed as a secretary to Hoederer in order to kill him, before the latter could implement his policy of collaboration. An intellectual, who became a Party member out of his hatred for his upper-class family and upbringing, he hesitated, feeling sympathy for Hoederer and wondering whether Hoederer's policy was not the right one, until he surprised his wife with Hoederer. Now he cannot decide whether he acted out of jealousy or political conviction.

In the last scene, he realizes that, while he was in prison, the Party line has changed, that Hoederer's policy is now official, and that he can be spared only if he forgets what he did, which, in the eyes of Olga, should be easy, since he is still wondering about his "real" motive. But he refuses to deny that what he did was devoid of political significance, that it can be erased: "You are asking me to be even more ashamed and decide that I killed him for nothing . . . Someone like Hoederer does not die by chance. He dies for his ideas, for his policy. He is responsible for his death . . . I still have not killed Hoederer, Olga. Not yet. It is now that I am going to kill him and myself too" (pp. 253-254). He attempts to give a definite and definitive meaning to what he did, not by determining the "real" motive, but by refusing to be spared.

*   *   *

Technically, *Dirty Hands* is interesting in that, between the first and last scenes, the purpose of the development is to enact what Hugo is remembering, and telling Olga. However, this is not quite accurate: there is a dialogue between Olga and Hugo's wife, Jessica, which takes place while Hugo is present, but asleep; and there are two dialogues, between Hoederer and Jessica, which take place in Hugo's absence. Sartre needs these scenes in order to give a comprehensive picture of past events. But they are technical faults nonetheless, since they cannot purport to dramatize Hugo's memories. And the dialogues between Jessica and Hoederer are the worst scenes of the play. Another bothersome detail is the placing of a fictional country, Illyria, in a precise geographical and historical frame. This kind of problem would not arise if historical pegs were dispensed with. The name of the country was dropped in a 1964 Italian adaptation of the play.

Dirty Hands provides a good example, the best one perhaps, of Sartre's ability to create suspense. In the outer play, the question is whether Hugo will be executed by his former companions at the end. In the inner play, the question is how and when (rather than whether) Hugo will kill Hoederer. The two questions are linked. At first, Hugo's fate appears to depend on how he will tell his story. He tells it in such a way that Olga is relieved: Hugo may be spared. But the effect of Olga's words on Hugo is to alter the link in two ways. It is what Hugo is going to do now that will determine the status of his past behavior: "I still have not killed Hoederer." And he will choose to die, rather than being spared: "It is now that I am going to kill Hoederer and myself too."

Retroactivity is thus stressed: the physical facts may already have been established, but the meaning of past behavior depends on present and future decisions. It is in vain that Hugo tries to decide what his motives were, what was really his objective, when he pressed the trigger, through recollection and introspection. The decision to cooperate or die is what will provide his past gesture with "motives" long after the fact. This is how historiography is written and rewritten.

Actually, Hugo's decision aims at a deeper transfiguration: what appears to him as pure gesture might be turned into a utilitarian action. Throughout the play, there are indications that Hugo has the impression of playing a theatrical role. In the middle of a conversation, he asks Jessica: "Are we playing or are we not?" (p. 112). It is suggested that, to a great extent, the impression of playing a role stems from the fact that Hugo refused the social destiny which was "naturally" designated for him, as the son of a rich bourgeois and as an intellectual. His fellow-communists make him feel that, despite his good will and determination, he is simply playing communist. Olga gave him the Romantic pseudonym of Raskolnikov. And Hoederer tells him: "An intellectual is not a real revolutionary" (p. 206). Hugo himself says: "Nothing ever seems quite real to me" (p. 112), and: "I am living in a theatrical setting" (p. 127). Besides, he is only playing the role of Hoederer's secretary. Half-drunk, Hugo generalizes his impression, applies it to various functions which he interprets as roles: "The head of a family is never really the head of a family. A murderer is never completely a murderer. They play, don't you understand? While a dead man is really dead . . . There is nothing I can be except a dead man with six feet of earth above his head. I am telling you, this is all comedy" (p. 162). These words are confirmed in the last scene when Hugo, before choosing to die, says: "I shot Hoederer in order to save the tragedy . . . Yes, I really moved a finger. Actors too move fingers, on stage" (pp. 219, 242).

A person is an agent (he, or it, functions) and an actor (he, or she, gestures). If gestures are divorced from utilitarian functioning, he play-acts. He may enjoy play-acting for its own sake. This is not the case with Hugo; it is not the case with other Sartrean characters: they do not want to play, they want to work. An unreasonable ambition for a theatrical ghost. Hugo despairs of the possibility of reconciling gesture and utilitarian function. So he thinks of death: a corpse functions chemically, gestures are gone.

Hugo kills Hoederer. In retrospect, he cannot see this action as a utilitarian incarnation. He cannot decide what the motive was; and what Olga tells him about the switch in policy relegates Hoederer and the murder of Hoederer to the realm of ineffectual theatrical gestures. What about committing suicide (letting himself be killed)? A corpse simply functions chemically, but committing suicide is an activity which may be given utilitarian purposes. Hoederer plus murder will be restored to the utilitarian field. The reflexive aspect of *Dirty Hands* is thus completed. The actor who plays Hugo ceases to be pure gestures when he disappears offstage (where Hugo is killed).

This is the end of the play. So the spectators or readers are not shown what meaning the other characters gave Hugo's suicide. Since the effect is not shown, one may start wondering about Hugo's "real" motive. Did he "really" hope to impose his own utilitarian interpretation, as told to Olga? Or did his words serve to conceal from himself the intention simply to become a politically meaningless corpse? What practical difference would different interpretations of his suicide by others make anyway? His words to Olga may be one more piece of play-acting. He simply wants to impress her with the well-played role of someone who goes as far as suicide to prove to himself, or pretend, he has utilitarian intentions. Does he even do that? I had better stop. The play leaves each spectator free to decide which "real" motive he likes best.

*   *   *

Dirty Hands was first performed in 1948. After some hesitations, it was more or less agreed in Parisian circles to make the play pass for a criticism of the Communist Party, or Parties. The anti-communist label may have contributed to making *Dirty Hands* the most successful (financially) of Sartre's plays. It is the play most often named by informants in an enquiry conducted in 1975 (*Obliques 18-19,* pp. 335-341).

At the time of the first performances, Sartre had declared that he did not take sides in favor of Hugo or Hoederer, idealism or realism: "A good play must present problems, not solve them" (*Un Théâtre de Situations,* p. 247). In the early fifties, during the cold war, he (vainly) attempted to draw closer to the Communist Party. He forbade performances of *Dirty Hands* in several places, in particular in Vienna, where a Peace Congress was to be held. But, while he had killed Hugo in the play, Sartre did not manage to kill the play (nor himself). What he did do was to stop the publication of the fourth volume of the novel *Roads of Freedom,* which contains indications of sudden inversions in the policies of the Communist Party.

In 1954, he deplored the fact his play had been "misused," and had become "an instrument of political propaganda" (*Les Ecrits de Sartre,* p. 182). In 1964, he told an interviewer: "The meaning of the play does not coincide with Hugo's destiny . . . I feel great comprehension for the attitude of Hugo, but you are wrong in thinking he embodies me. I embody myself in Hoederer. Ideally, of course: do not think I claim to be Hoederer" (*Les Ecrits de Sartre,* p. 183).

These developments are full of dramatic irony. The author of *What is Literature?* attempts to unite his audience, except for the Communist faithful. An impish genie grants his wish, but in a way Sartre does not relish. He dislikes the kind of propaganda that he believes the play has been made to serve.

One of the lessons of the play is that to find a "real" motive is to invent it. Yet Sartre, in the 1964 interview, speaks of the "real meaning" (*vrai sens*) of his play, that is to say, the meaning (he now says) he wanted to give it, instead of recognizing that a play has the significance anyone chooses to give it.

On the other hand, he does recognize an "objective" meaning, the practical use ("misuse") to which the play was put as anti-communist propaganda. We may recall his summary judgement: "I wrote exactly the contrary of what I wanted to write." That is to say: he decides he wrote the contrary of what he decides he wanted to write.

But, in 1956, Sartre protested against the Russian intervention in Hungary; and, after that, he became reconciled to the idea that the French Communist Party was a conservative force. Indeed, it provides some Frenchmen with a sense of belonging to a venerable family and, at the same time, with a possibility of playing criticism and revolt without the risk of having to take power and assume the burden of governing a country. These days, the comedian most often on display on French bourgeois television is the secretary of the Communist Party.

"It's all a comedy," says Hugo. In his comments on the play, Sartre forgets to include Hoederer among the comedians. In his attempts to kill the play, he took seriously the "misuse" that had been made of it. To a detached spectator, it appears that this too was part of a show, part of politics yes, but only to the extent that political dialectic generates theatrical froth. What matters happens offstage. No doubt, from a cognitive standpoint, not only the wings, but also the stage, are part of the historical field. But too little is known about brains to establish laws governing relations between the two areas. All I can do is formulate my reactions and make a few assumptions about others.

If Sartre did not want the meaning of the play to coincide with Hugo's destiny, why did he make Hugo the main character, the object of the double suspense, the character who faces death at the end, and whose memories the inner play is supposed to dramatize? If he wanted Hoederer to appear in a better light than Hugo, why did he let Hoederer put on airs of superiority, adopt a paternalistic attitude toward other characters, especially Hugo? Why did he let him talk demagogically, and gratuitously, about his love of men "for what they are" (p. 205), forgetting to add what he hated them for? What is the symptomatic meaning of this verbal gesture? Is it that Hoederer likes Racine and that he has read somewhere that Racine, unlike Corneille, depicts men "as they really are"?

In *The Theatre of Jean-Paul Sartre* (p. 73), Dorothy McCall opines that Hoederer "has transcended gestures." Was she influenced by what Sartre thought it proper to say in the passage of the 1964 interview quoted above?

There is an attempt, in the play, to set Hoederer on a pedestal of "reality." Hugo says that Hoederer's coffee-pot "looks real when he touches it" and that "everything that he touches looks real" (p. 127). And the frivolous Jessica tells Hoederer: "You are real. A real man of flesh and bones" (p. 34). Meaning that a surgeon can operate on him? These words are intended to contrast with Hugo's impression that he himself is only playing.

But, on the other hand, Hugo generalizes at one point his impression of comedy. And, at the end, he realizes that Hoederer's actions have been reduced to gestures. As for the coffee-pot, it may indeed look "real" to spectators. But this simply means that a real coffee-pot is used as a prop, which would be better integrated in the dramatic dialectic if it turned into a bewitched tool, or rather toy, squirting ink at the faces of babbling characters.

If the flesh and bones of Hoederer, not of the historical actor, are "real" to the spectators, they are no longer watching a play. And the flesh and bones of Hugo will be just as "real." In the case of Hoederer, Sartre may have attempted to suggest utilitarian actions involving drudgery and risks of physical suffering to many. But all we have is verbal gestures (and the explosion of a petard at one point). Dramas have a more restricted range of possibilities of esthetic conversion than novels or films.

THE DEVIL AND THE GOOD LORD (1951)

Act I, first tableau. The archbishop of Worms learns of the victory of his troops over the troops of Conrad, a rebellious vassal, who has been killed. The scene shifts to Worms, which has also rebelled against the archbishop. It is besieged by the troops of Goetz, the illegitimate brother of Conrad. Goetz has betrayed Conrad and allied himself with the archbishop. Inside Worms, Nasty, the leader of the poor, tries to counteract the effect of the news of Conrad's defeat. The scene shifts back to the archbishop's palace. The archbishop and a banker discuss how Goetz could be persuaded to spare Worms, in whose prosperity both the archbishop and the banker are interested. In the famished city, Heinrich, a priest, tries to fight Nasty's influence over the people. The bishop (not be be confused with the archbishop, who is not in Worms) is besieged by the people within the city. He reminds Heinrich that he

has to choose between the people and his allegiance to the Church. Nasty
persuades the people that the bishop is concealing reserves of grain. Riot.
Before dying the bishop entrusts Heinrich with the key to an underground
passage which will allow Goetz to take the city. Heinrich is to surrender
Worms on condition that Goetz spare the priests.

Second tableau. Goetz's camp. Goetz takes pleasure in tormenting
Heinrich, who cannot bring himself to reveal the secret entrance. Goetz points
out to Heinrich the similarity of their positions: they are both outcasts. He
advises Heinrich to imitate him: "Choose Evil." Goetz learns of Conrad's
death. Heinrich then perceives that Goetz loathes himself. He gives the key to
Goetz. Now it is Goetz's responsibility.

Third tableau. Goetz's tent. Catherine, his mistress, discovers an officer
who has been lying in ambush to kill Goetz. Catherine hides him in the tent: she
will give him the signal to kill Goetz if she chooses. Goetz arrives. He tells
Catherine that he is going to receive Conrad's estate and that he will take her
with him. The banker arrives. He tries to persuade Goetz to spare Worms.
Goetz refuses his bribes. The banker is taken away. Goetz has changed his
mind: he will abandon Catherine. She gives the signal to the hidden officer,
but changes her mind at once and warns Goetz in time. The officer is disarmed
and taken away. Nasty arrives. He had left Worms to raise a peasant army,
but, upon learning that Worms had been betrayed, he has surrendered to
Goetz's soldiers. He offers Goetz the generalship of the poor. Goetz refuses
this temptation of "the Good." He has Heinrich brought in, so that the latter
may confess his enemy, Nasty. Heinrich and Nasty insult each other.
Meanwhile, Goetz is getting ready to invade the city. But Heinrich finally
succeeds where the banker, Catherine, and Nasty, had failed. He does not
tempt Goetz with the Good, but tells him that everyone does Evil, as does
Goetz, since to do the Good is impossible. Goetz's Luciferian pride is hurt. He
wagers against Heinrich that the Good can be done. He subordinates his
decision between Good and Evil to a dice throw, but cheats in order that the
dice may enjoin him to do the Good. He decides to spare Worms. He will meet
Heinrich in one year so that the latter may decide whether Goetz has won his
bet or not.

Act II, fourth tableau. The scene is laid in Conrad's estate, Heidenstamm, which has been given to Goetz. Goetz is practicing Christian love and
charity. Not only the barons, but also Nasty, try in vain to persuade him not to
distribute his land to the peasants. This gesture will incite the peasants to revolt
everywhere. And Nasty thinks that these spontaneous uprisings will be
premature.

Fifth tableau. In Heidenstamm, the peasants themselves do not respond to Goetz's gesture as he had hoped. They still think in the framework of the old order. Tetzel, a seller of indulgences, provides Goetz with a lesson in popular psychology. Heinrich, who now imagines that a devil dogs his steps, and pretends to be possessed, tells Goetz that Catherine is in the neighborhood, dying. Goetz leaves in search of Catherine. Heinrich proposes to Nasty a scheme to prevent premature uprisings in the whole country: the priests will leave their parishes and abscond, thus paralyzing with fear the minds of the peasants. A realist, Nasty accepts.

Sixth tableau. Peasants have taken refuge in a church, in the absence of their priest. Heinrich's plan has succeeded. Goetz arrives. He has learned that Catherine is dying in this church. Hilda, the daughter of a rich miller, has been devoting her life to the poor. She has been taking care of the dying Catherine. The latter, a prey to infernal visions, implores Goetz to save her. Goetz asks God to make him a scapegoat for Catherine's sins. As no sign descends from heaven, he pierces his hands and presents his wounds as divine stigmata to Catherine, who dies in peace, and to the peasants, who accept him as a prophet.

Act III, seventh tableau. Goetz has established a perfect Christian community. The peasants are taught universal love and nonviolence. Hilda feels she has been robbed by Goetz's success. Meanwhile, in other parts of the country, the peasants have started a revolt against the lords. Nasty asks Goetz to take command of the peasant army.

Eighth and ninth tableaux. The camp of Nasty's army. Goetz advises the peasants not to fight: they do not have a chance. In order to persuade them, he takes advantage of his reputation as a prophet. But Karl, his former servant, who hates him, beats Goetz at his own game. Goetz leaves the camp and decides to forget about saving men. During his absence, a group of peasants, infuriated by the refusal of Goetz's people to join them in their revolt, have killed everyone in sight. Hilda is the only survivor. Goetz is confirmed in his decision to become a masochistic hermit.

Tenth tableau. One year after the start of the play, Heinrich arrives, accompanied by his personal devil, in order to judge whether Goetz has won his bet. But, instead of playing the role of the Pharisee, as Heinrich had expected, Goetz plays the role of the Publican, and even the role of prosecutor when Heinrich proves unequal to the task. The exchange between the two characters exposes the comedy they have been playing. Goetz does not believe in his god any more than Heinrich believes in his devil. Heinrich cannot tolerate this disclosure of metaphysical emptiness. The two men fight. Heinrich is killed. Goetz announces to Hilda that God is dead.

Eleventh tableau. The camp of Nasty's army. Despite his repugnance, Nasty lets a witch restore confidence in his men: the application of a magic talisman is supposed to make them invulnerable. Goetz arrives with Hilda. He would like to enlist as a soldier, so as to avoid responsibility. But Nasty needs a general, not soldiers. Goetz accepts. He lets the witch minister to him. He accepts the responsibility of a general: he kills an officer who has challenged his authority. He accepts a situation which he did not choose: "There is a war to be fought and I shall fight it."

*   *   *

Among Sartre's plays, *Le Diable et le Bon Dieu* (hereafter *The Devil*) is the most ambitious, the most complex, the richest in events. Like *The Flies, Dirty Hands, Altona,* it may be called a Romantic drama. And it offers a Romantic (Hegelian) aspect which is absent from the other plays: a clear dialectic of opposites structuring the evolution of the hero. Goetz switches from the pursuit of pure Evil to the pursuit of pure Goodness. Positive and collective at first (the creation of a community with Christianlike slogans), his quest for the Good becomes negative and personal (masochistic asceticism). In the final stage, he appears to drop allegories, at least those of Good and Evil, perhaps not that of Man.

The dialectical development may strike one as too clear-cut and overloaded with allegorical grandiloquence. But *The Devil* is at least Sartre's play which raises metamoral questions most acutely. Before turning to such questions, I shall point out connections of *The Devil* with *Saint Genet* and *The Words.* I shall also question its relevance to a contemporary situation.

*   *   *

Saint Genet corresponds to *The Devil* as *Being and Nothingness* and *Existentialism is a Humanism* correspond to *The Flies.* But it is to be recalled that the equation of Being with the Good already occurs for the first time in *The Flies,* when Jupiter identifies himself and what he created with Being and Goodness.

"We *are* not and we *have* nothing" (p. 55). Goetz, the illegitimate son of a noblewoman, likens his situation to that of Heinrich, a priest torn between his allegiance to the Church and his duty to the people. Goetz's situation has been imposed upon him; now he wills it, overplays it, tries to appropriate it: "We are not inside the world. We are outside! Refuse this world which does not want you. Choose Evil" (p. 55). In a social order which tends to identify Goodness with being through having, Evil can but be a lack. Compare what Sartre says of Genet:

> He assumes and projects before him the curse which, from the depths of his past, from the past of his mother, rises to the present: it will be his future. It was imposed on him: he turns it into a mission . . . He needed rules, precepts, advice; he loved the constraint of the Good: he will build a black system of ethics with precepts and rules, with uncompromising restraints, a Jansenism of Evil. But he will not reject, for all that, the crude theological morality of men of property: it is on this conception of morals that his system of values will be grafted and will grow like a cancer. (*Saint Genet,* p. 56)

Seeking for the worst, Goetz, like Sartre's Genet, chooses betrayal. The gesture has a symbolic sparkle which delights him: "Of course bastards are traitors, what else could they be? I am a double agent by birth; my mother gave herself to a peasant and I am made up of two halves which do not fit" (p. 55).

Destruction is a necessary means of construction. But Goetz is fascinated by his negative situation. He tries to appropriate a state of affairs through destruction only. His pride is Luciferian. Similarly, Sartre presents Genet as converting utilitarian activities into allegorical role playing:

> He wants action. But he falls back at once into his obsession: he wants to do in order to be, to steal in order to be the robber, to do Evil in order to be the Evil-doer . . . An action which is accomplished in order to *be* is no longer an action,

but a gesture . . . Thus Evil is not the absolute end of his projects, it is the means
he has chosen to represent his "nature" to himself. But if he does not *do* Evil, he
is not an evil-doer; he plays the role of the evil-doer. (*Saint Genet*, p. 75)

It is Heinrich who shatters Goetz's theatrical pose: Goetz is but a
buffoon of the devil; does he believe that he will be the only one to be damned?
Besides, is he even sure to be damned? God might play the trick of forgiveness
on him, thus erasing the meaning which Goetz wants his gestures to have in the
eyes of God, the only spectator and critic Goetz considers worthy of him.

Heinrich contends that to do the Good is impossible. Goetz accepts the
challenge of his alter ego. An excerpt from *Saint Genet* will serve as a
comment on Goetz's abrupt metamorphosis: "Saint Martin, Saint George,
Saint Ignatius, in our time Father de Foucauld, who will probably be
canonized, show how easily one can pass from the military condition to
sainthood" (*Saint Genet*, p. 190).

Goetz gives away the lands he has been granted. But his charitable
gesture would become a benefic activity only if the peasants responded
appropriately. His good has somehow to be recognized as such by the
peasants: "Nobody can choose the good of others in their place" (p. 135).
Goetz is rejected by the peasants as Orestes was rejected by the Argives.
Tetzel, the seller of indulgences, is loved by the peasants through the magic of
myth. And the only person who has ever loved Goetz, through the magic of
flesh, is the dying Catherine. Goetz takes advantage of these lessons. He
pierces his hands and presents his wounds to Catherine, then to the peasants,
as divine stigmata. Catherine dies in peace and the peasants are won over:
"They are mine. At last" (p. 166). Goetz can now play the role of prophet.

Childishly, the peasants are taught to love all men and practice
nonviolence. At least, they enjoy a life of material and psychological peace, or
slumber. But this comparative success is soon denied. A group of armed
peasants, angered by the refusal of Goetz's people to join them in their
struggle, destroy the village and slaughter its peaceful inhabitants.

The destruction of Goetz's paradise on earth, and the refusal of Nasty's
army to listen to Goetz when he urges them not to fight, lead the hero to adopt a
new role: that of masochistic hermit and would-be mystic. He tries to leave
men alone and return to a dialogue with a hidden god which shows he has read
John of the Cross:

There we are, Lord. We are face to face again, as in the good old days when I was doing evil. I should never have meddled with men: they are a nuisance. They are the brushwood one must push aside in order to come to you. I am coming to you, Lord, I am coming; I am walking in your night; lend me your hand. Tell me: the night, it is you, isn't it? Night, the harrowing absence of everything! For you are the one who is present in universal absence, the one who is heard when all is silence . . . Until I possess everything, I shall possess nothing. Until I am everything, I shall be nothing (p. 201).

As a masochistic hermit, Goetz has turned his talent to the role of the Publican, who tries to transform the plurality of egos into a duality: breast and hand, sinner and judge. The sinner is condemned, not the judge. But it is the others who hold the key to our "objectivity": "I need someone to judge me. Every day, every hour, I condemn myself, but I cannot manage to convince myself because I know myself too well to trust myself. I do not see my soul because it is right under my nose. I need someone who would lend me his eyes" (p. 220). The fact that the allegorical addressee, God, remains silent was convenient; now it has become a drawback.

Heinrich, who has wagered against Goetz that the Good cannot be done, is only too glad to oblige. But he is disconcerted by Goetz's willingness to condemn himself, so that Goetz is obliged to prompt him and assume the other's role. The judgment scene has the effect of an exorcism. Capitalized verbal idols (God, Being and Non-Being, Good and Evil) disappear. Unlike Orestes, Goetz accepts the "throne" Nasty offers him. But this decision does not bring him psychologically closer to the peasants than Orestes was to the Argives.

*   *   *

In *The Words,* Sartre recalls that, as a child, he loved adventure stories and that he preferred "the adventurer to the intellectual" (*Les Mots,* p. 147). In the character of Goetz, adventurer and intellectual are united. Sartre lists *Goetz von Berlichingen* as one of his early readings. He adds that he has always been inclined to dream of life in the perspective of an "epic idealism" (*Les Mots,* p. 101).

This epic idealism goes with his impression that he was given a mandate. But, at the same time, "I could neither draw from myself the imperative mandate which would have justified my presence on earth, nor grant to anyone the right to give it to me" (*Les Mots,* p. 114). In *The Devil,* Nasty claims a divine mandate: "I received a mandate to go and speak to you" (p. 85). Goetz too claims that mandates are given to him, but: "I can't tell who gave them to me." His behavior will be ambiguous. He will pretend that God ordered him to do the Good by a throw of the dice, but Catherine will say that he cheated. He will pierce his hands and pretend that it is a miracle. Finally, in the judgment scene with Heinrich, he will agree that he gave himself orders: "There was only I; I alone decided about Evil; I alone invented the Good" (p. 228). These words echo the principle that each person has to choose moral goals. Nobody is God; but everyone has to act (or play-act) as if he were God, since everyone has to decide what will happen and what will be best, against a background of uncertainty.

The following extract from *The Words* has already been quoted in the comments on *The Flies:* "I was told that the characters of my plays and novels make their decisions abruptly, in a crisis, that, for instance, Orestes, in *The Flies,* needs only a moment to achieve his conversion. Naturally: it is because I create them in my own image, not as I am, of course, but as I wanted to be" (*Les Mots,* p. 199). Goetz, with his sudden shifts in behavior, would be a better example than Orestes.

At the time of *The Devil,* Sartre seems to have liked to think of himself as a traitor to his class, the bourgeoisie. Goetz is also presented as such a traitor. And the following passage from *The Words* may bring to mind Goetz's switches: "Though I devote myself entirely to what I undertake, to work, anger, friendship, in a moment, I shall deny myself, I know it, I want it, and I betray myself already in the midst of passion, with the joyful presentiment of my future treason" (*Les Mots,* pp. 199-200). Sartre also talks about his willingness to acknowledge his mistakes with good grace, thus irritating his accuser (*Les Mots,* p. 201). The passage may recall the judgment scene, in which Goetz frustrates Heinrich by accusing himself. If you play goalkeeper you should not also try to play center forward for the other team.

In *The Words,* Sartre speaks of the dream of a personal, and collective, progress proceeding by abrupt and radical leaps. He adds: "Of course, I am not blind: I can see that we repeat ourselves. But this more recently acquired knowledge corrodes my old intuitions without dissipating them entirely" (*Les Mots,* p. 202). He likes psychological *coups de théâtre,* that tend to deny set personalities. But, in *The Devil,* the result of Goetz's jerky evolution is that he returns to his first role, that of a ruthless condotierre, with different words to clothe it.

I have already noted that, in *The Words,* Sartre considers atheism "a long and cruel task," which he believes he has finally accomplished (*Les Mots,* p.212). This is not to say, of course, that the itinerary of Goetz parallels that of Sartre. All I can say is that there are myth-making propensities in Sartre's uses of some words. In *Being and Nothingness,* nothingness is like a conjurer's hat (see: nothing in it) from which the rabbit of temporality is extracted, also the dove of freedom, which turns into the vulture of responsibility. I am reminded of Hegelian alchemy: becoming as the synthesis of being and non-being. The medieval equation of Good with Being, Evil with Nothingness, is adopted in *Saint Genet. Being and Nothingness* announces a morals of "salvation." The redemptive treatise of morals was not published (some notes came out recently: see *Obliques 18-19).* Instead of that, *Saint Genet* offers the dream of a "synthesis" of Good-Being and Nothingness-Evil, impossible today. *The Words* concludes: "If I put aside impossible salvation, what remains ? A whole man, made up of all men, as good as, and no better than, anybody else" (*Les Mots,* p. 214). I still suspect an allegorical figure in this totalization of all men in one man. In *The Devil,* Goetz is content to display a modest (and vacuous) resolution simply to be "a man among men."

In a note on Husserl, written in the nineteen thirties, Sartre had added "thing among things" to "man among men" (*Situations,* I, 35). Not only other animal species, but also things, seem to have disappeared from the landscape.

Theoretically, the historical field is one. So any historical event may be taken to be the product of all other previous events (within the speed of light, according to the current physical model). For instance, I have traced my lineage back to two pterodactyls named Adam and Eve. Why single out anthropomorphic creatures? And why dump all of them into each of them?

The Parisians of Montesquieu exclaimed: "How can one be a Persian?" Sometimes I wonder how one can be a Sartre. Differences between back- grounds. On my side, an easy-going pagan Catholicism in my childhood milieu, with strictly functional saints the Vatican had never heard of, plus mildly haunted houses and a few witch-doctors popping up here and there and disappearing. This was close to the birthplace of Descartes; but no big Evil Genius manifested itself. Also a fairly illiterate milieu (how can Sartre intimate that, as a child, he had decided to *be* a writer?). But, above all, differences between temperaments.

*   *   *

Connections between *The Devil* and a contemporary situation are obvious in the case of Heinrich. Worker-priests were in the news at the time. The analogy between Nasty and a leader of the French Communist Party is less apt.

The peasants in *The Devil* cannot be made to correspond to French farmers or agricultural workers in the middle of the twentieth century. French peasants were revolutionary fuel in 1789, not in 1950. The peasants in the play may be likened, not to French urban or rural workers, but to peasants in countries whose economy was still predominantly agricultural in 1950: China, for instance. It was in such countries that revolutions continued to take place. In 1871, the Commune, limited to Paris, had failed. In May 1968, the student revolt in Paris made practical sense as far as reforms in universities were concerned. The rest was a nostalgic show. One might think of small terrorist groups or of revolts in East European countries. But this is not what *The Devil* prophesies.

What about the character of Goetz? Surely, Sartre was not thinking of Charles de Gaulle, though the latter was something of a hermit at the time. Did Sartre think that he himself might be offered the leadership of Communist troops in France? This is ridiculous. But was not *Mein Kampf* considered a joke by most people at the beginning? The situation was quite different; it is also doubtful that the book helped the rise of the Nazi movement significantly; finally, *Saint Genet* and *The Devil* do not look like *Mein Kampf.* More generally, in collective phenomena such as the feminine movement for instance, are fiction and literary criticism more than icing on a cake, foam on a beach, shimmering wavelets on a stream? Fugitive, confused, confusing; dazzling, blinding.

In *The Devil* , the peasants are presented as stupid, like the Argives in *The Flies.* Does the play suggest that Sartre despaired of enlightening a broad popular audience? On the average, manual workers are not more silly than intellectuals. In the play, the superstitions of the peasants are not more stupid drugs than the rhetoric of Goetz.

But the play can integrate the peasants only as crowds, as choruses. Choruses are stupid; sometimes, beautifully stupid or stupidly beautiful. Grouping does not always make everybody stupider than anybody in every respect. An average physicist profits from the genius of Maxwell, Einstein, or Dirac. Political grouping is another matter. Each member has to stultify himself, to the extent he is a member. Or pretend to; practically, the result is the same. Even at the top. Some central committee may take a decision unanimously, of which each participant disapproves in petto. Each participant is afraid of sounding like a traitor.

During a dramatic performance, must spectators play stupid in order to let a contagious effect take place and unite them in a uniform chorus? Diverse reactions do not necessarily ruin a show. They may enrich the ludic world, instead of disrupting it. Some spectators may be amused by the overt reactions of some others, instead of resenting them.

"The men of today," says Goetz in the last scene, "are born criminals" (p. 235). Are spectators and readers expected to understand "sixteenth century," or "twentieth century," or both? What is the difference with other periods? Same question for evocations of superstition, myth-making, religiosity.

* * *

The notion that humans are born criminals recalls the principle of existential shame laid down in *Being and Nothingness,* i.e. the Sartrean version of the original sin. But *The Devil,* more particularly the behavior of Goetz, shows the insufficiency of this principle. To account for cruelty (to oneself and others), it would be convenient to lay down a principle of existential rancor. Of course, the accounting I am speaking of is philosophical. Scientifically, it is worthless. Rancor is not an experimental variable.

Someone may be ashamed of the superfluity of his incarnated existence, and try to justify it. But he may also resent the fact that he was embodied in this vale of tears, without being asked. One need not be a bastard like Goetz in order to be called a bastard in an insulting sense. If someone does not consider suicide a sufficient vengeance, he will have to try to stay alive in order to avenge himself for being alive. A lot of explanatory mileage can be squeezed out of this formula. A lot, though not all the mileage that is needed to be comprehensive (and play fair). Every tankful has limits. For all I know, there may be people lucky and insensitive enough to manage to view the vale of tears as a playing field. And every kind of energy must bow to entropy. To a thermodynamically minded reader, the denouement of *The Devil* (denouement: *analusis,* deliverance, dissolution) would suggest entropy, battle fatigue, not a Hegelian kind of redemption (*sunthesis*).

In *Violence et Ethique* (p. 138), Pierre Verstraeten interprets the final verbal gestures of Goetz as a "conversion of the adventurer (hero-saint) to praxis." *Praxis* is a label adopted by Sartre, and some Marxists, to cover utilitarian activities, at least those which involve a lot of people and group dialectic. Phonetically, its consonants combine the roughness of *pratique* and *action.* So it is more impressive.

What is praxis in the case of Goetz? Apparently participating in a collective war, as general, not as a soldier. Which is what he was doing in the first place. Wars involve killing. Those who oppose your moral convictions must be won over or eliminated. Add euthanasia.

Detached playing fields are many. Theoretically, the historical field is one. Practically, it is one to the extent it has the unity of a stinking battlefield. How is it that humans (unfortunately?) have not destroyed the human species already, let alone others? Lack of moral convictions. Fatigue. Zones of agreement. Uncertainty. Fear of retaliation: I have got to stay alive in order to keep avenging myself for being alive.

Respect of rules for the sake of respecting rules. Uniqueness is experienced. It can also be thought as the opposite of anythingness. But the uniqueness of a state of affairs, or a goal, cannot be thought. We can only think repetitions, classify singular events, frame singularities with generalities. So we need natural laws, rules of behavior, human and nonhuman, that make it appear that moral activities are rule-governed ludic activities.

To cut the enumeration short: fear of suffering, for oneself. And for others: let us not be too cynical. A lot of skepticism and cynicism is needed to philosophize; but not too much. Otherwise, philosophizing itself would be denied.

"Thou shalt not kill." What does someone who makes this verbal gesture think that his biological defense mechanisms are doing in order to allow him to assume this role? Well, he does not mean that germs must not be killed. Does he mean one must not kill flies, or oxen, or whales? Perhaps not: only anthropomorphic creatures. Because the speaker believes he belongs to this category? Because some of them speak English? Parrots and computers can be made to say "Thou shalt not kill" or "*Cogito ergo sum.*" Human life is sacred. Human life (not this or that life) is an allegory. Allegories are what can be sacred. Consecrated.

I have heard that "Thou shalt not kill" is the motto of Cruelty International (a secret society): make your victim last as long as possible. If we lay down the metamoral principle that grave suffering, suffering that cannot be alleviated, that cannot be terminated except by death, is the limit of moral antisense, death is not by itself a moral antivalue. Conditions may be such that killing (oneself or others) is the only resort. To kill someone painlessly at time t1 may prevent him from dying at time t7 after long suffering. Ecologists want to preserve species. So that new individuals may add their suffering?

Hypocrisy is to social functioning what oil is to a combustion engine. Without hypocrisy (and some self-hypocrisy), one cannot survive for twenty-four hours, except by being locked up. Which reminds me I am no longer six years old. We need to survive some time in order to avenge ourselves for being alive. And also to do some good. Or play. Some societies allow their members, or some of their members, to lighten the burden of hypocrisy in some ludic activities. Writing an essay for instance.

The paragraphs that precede sketch a definition of moral values and antivalues. Someone else may prefer a different decoupage. If this happens, I may be unable to decide whether I am dealing with hypocrisy or the expression of a different temperament. Furthermore, two persons may adopt the same theoretical principles and disagree as to what should be done in a particular case, because suffering is not a scientific variable that could be measured with portable meters and predicted. This is an example of what makes philosophizing appear pointless. But also innocuous. The same cannot be said for scientific experimentation and technology. Philosophy is semantic surgery. Sometimes, one has the impression of operating on marsh water.

Let us concentrate on the last words of Goetz, and of the play: "There is this war to be fought and I shall fight it." He is not in favor of this war, but it cannot be avoided. And he prefers to participate in it on the side of the peasant army. He says he would prefer to be a soldier, but he is needed as the best general available.

It is suggested that he is not in favor of the war, because the peasants have no chance of winning. In this case, since he is supposed to be the best general, his participation should prolong the war. So his perspective is ludic: there is this war game to be played, and if he plays general, it will be played better. To be certain of losing does not always make one play badly. A soccer team may surpass itself when it is outclassed. Goetz just has to allow the peasants to believe that they can win.

Suppose now Goetz thinks that the peasants do not have a chance, that his being their general will prolong war, but that he is no longer interested in playing general. If he assumes the role, there will be more killing, suffering, torturing, maiming. Why does he accept? To make a show of solidarity in the eyes of Nasty, Hilda, and above all himself? His final verbal gestures make this interpretation the most likely.

The kind of war evoked in *The Devil* would be called "conventional" now. In such wars, there is a tacit rule that the killing will be limited, so that suffering may prosper. Another factor which diminishes the relevance of the play is that the setting prevents it from mentioning features of modern technology such as anesthetic drugs, and ultimate weapons. Goetz does not have a choice between total murder-suicide and limited killing plus preservation of suffering. Nor is he allowed to say: "I do not have ultimate weapons at my disposal. So I had better not play general, for this could only produce more suffering in a war which cannot be won by the side I like."

On the other hand, a decision to lead the peasant army might be defended in this way: "There is going to be a lot of suffering, and the war will last longer if I act as general. But there will at least be much more killing. Those who thus die sooner will not suffer later and will have no chance of avenging themselves for being alive by producing more children."

Suppose now Goetz thinks that the peasant army can win the war, especially with him as general. He might also think a peasant victory would produce social and economic conditions that would be morally less unfavorable.

I have sketched a few perspectives in which a moral decision could be taken in a situation such as that of Goetz. But his verbal gestures, and those of others, are favorable only to the first two perspectives: either Goetz wants the war game to be played better thanks to his leadership; or, more conspicuously, he wants to make a show of solidarity in the eyes of a few, especially himself. Both perspectives are ludic; the second is more precisely theatrical. So, the term "praxis," as I understand it (utilitarian activity), would not fit the last metamorphosis of Goetz.

Why is this metamorphosis the end of the play rather than the beginning? Because a protracted shadow-boxing with theological idols made for more flamboyant drama than war strategy and tactic on stage? Catholic reviewers reacted to the Christian baits as they were expected to. And quite a few spectators may have decided to attend one of the first performances to hear how the word *Dieu* was treated, or mistreated. Whom does Goetz represent in 1951 in Paris? Pierre Brasseur, of course, who created the role. This move would make relevance reduce to reflexivity.

KEAN (1953)

The differences between the play attributed to Dumas and Sartre's adaptation lie not so much in the plot as in the portrayal of Kean, the actor.

Whereas the character of Dumas says: "I play comedy from eight o'clock in the evening till midnight, but never during the day" (p. 291), Sartre was interested in the contamination of private life by profession. An actor whose life is invaded by play-acting attitudes may pass for a paradigm of the human condition as defined in *Being and Nothingness.* Self-hypocrisy is summarized in these words of Kean: "I am playing, I am not playing, I don't know" (p. 87). He cannot get rid of self-hypocrisy. But, thanks to the plurality of egos, a plurality sharpened by his profession, he can at least recognize it. Such overt recognitions are rare in daily life.

It is in *Kean* that reflexivity is most conspicuous. For instance: "There's nobody on the stage. Nobody. Or perhaps an actor playing Kean in the role of Othello" (p. 166). Similarly: "To play, you must take yourself for someone else. I took myself for Kean, who took himself for Hamlet, who took himself for Fortinbras" (p. 176).

A performance of a play offers at least three perspectives of interpretation: personification of a utilitarian actor, personification of ludic role (ludic Kean), personification of esthetic characters (Othello, Hamlet, Fortinbras). In *Kean,* the esthetic character is the character of a comedian.

It is usual to subordinate esthetic character to ludic role, and ludic role to historical individual. This is what happens in the quoted passages. Except, of course, that the historical-ludic-esthetic trilogy itself is enclosed within fictionalizing brackets.

Above, or below, the three types of signified individuals, there is "nobody." This "nobody" may recall the "nothingness" which characterizes impersonal consciousness in *Being and Nothingness.* Since I want to avoid getting mixed in being and nonbeing, I would prefer to say that, basically, there are experienced signs. Nonpersonified significations-interpretations are experienced, as well as the non-sensical ballast of signs. What is signified is to be thought, and as such not experienced. For instance, a narration plus personification may posit an historical actor; or it may posit a ludic role, or an esthetic character. An allegorical figure like God (or Man) shows an attempt to personify the transcendent domain. *Being and Nothingness* calls this domain "nothingness." I call it "experienced signs." Transcendent signs must not be reduced to a unity (divine *Verbum,* or *Logos*).

Like Hugo in *Dirty Hands,* Kean generalizes what is obvious in his own case: "Don't be afraid. It's only Kean, the actor, playing the role of Kean. What about you? You are playing the part of the Prince of Wales, are you not? . . . . Beware of the Countess of Koefeld. Of the three of us, she is the one who plays her part best" (p. 69).

The opposition between theatrical gesture and utilitarian action makes two appearances. "For twenty years, I have been making gestures to please you; do you understand that I might want really to act?" (p. 65). After insulting the Prince of Wales, Kean asks himself: "Was it a gesture or an action?" (p. 178). But the impression of being confined to a theatrical cave does not bother Kean as much as it bothered Hugo, or Garcin in *No Exit.* Kean, like Sartre, or a certain Sartre, is more light-hearted.

Like other Sartrean characters, Kean may be said to be motivated by pride: "I was sick with pride. Pride is the other side of shame" (p. 179). Here again one may recall the principle of existential shame and of a desire to justify one's existence. Shall we say that, added to grandiloquence, pride is enough to give a dramatic character a set personality, a *caractère?*

I see no particular connection between *Kean* and a contemporary French situation at the time of the first performances. According to Simone de Beauvoir, Sartre had "a lot of fun" adapting Dumas's play (*La Force des Choses,* p. 320). He must have enjoyed composing a character who could serve as a paradigm of a metadramatic conception of humans, without having to wonder anxiously about "praxis."

In *What is Literature?,* he assumed that people never undertake to compose fiction or essays (or poetry?) for the sake of playing with and against words. They would always attempt to "feel essential in relation to the world." And only the dream of being read, taken seriously, and interpreted in the way they want, by numerous other people, could sustain this project. They would think of prospective readers, attempt to guess and channel their reactions as if they were sending them business or love letters. Some readers may be inclined to reduce *What is Literature?* to a smokescreen or cloud of incense designed to conceal or glorify authorial vanity.

I would not make these sweeping assumptions. I would not even apply them to Sartre all the time. Reading his texts, it sometimes appears to me that he was not thinking of prospective readers while he was writing. Writing must have afforded him an escape from boredom and frustration, also a more positive pleasure like a sport. He was a professional player. But professional players often forget they are working. They play for the sake of playing.

NEKRASSOV (1955)

Georges de Valera, a distinguished swindler hunted by the police, makes a half-hearted attempt at suicide by drowning in the Seine, then takes refuge in Sibilot's apartment. Sibilot's daughter, Véronique, who works for a leftist newspaper, decides to protect Valera. Sibilot, who is in charge of anti-Soviet propaganda for *Soir à Paris,* has just been warned by Palotin, the editor-in-chief, that he will lose his job if he does not find some new gimmick. Valera provides it: he will play the part of Nekrassov, a Soviet dignitary who is rumored to have disappeared. Like Kravchenko, Valera-Nekrassov will have defected to the West.

The next day, Palotin and the directors of *Soir à Paris* are only too happy with the ready-made Nekrassov to question his identity. Valera-Nekrassov will reserve his declarations for *Soir à Paris.* But the situation soon begins to pall on the adventurer. He is confined to a hotel room with his bodyguards; his pseudorevelations cause several people employed by *Soir à Paris* to be fired; and additions are made to what he says, as a prelude to the arrest of two political friends of Véronique. She manages to see Valera and shows him that he has become a plaything in the hands of the people he is supposed to fool.

Matters come to a head at a party given by Mrs. Bounoumi, a Christian-Democrat politician. Valera manages to escape those who watch over him as Nekrassov and the police inspector who hunts him as Valera. He takes refuge again in Sibilot's apartment, tells Véronique he will give her an interview about how Georges de Valera became Nekrassov. In a kind of epilogue, the directors of *Soir à Paris* sacrifice Palotin and replace him with a remorse-stricken Sibilot.

*   *   *

Nekrassov is in the tradition of Aristophanes. Correlatively, it is Sartre's play which allows one most easily to give a precise sense to the theory of committed literature. The relevance is not blurred or dispersed by a setting distant in time. The play refers to the Kravchenko case and to the cold war propaganda practiced in Parisian newspapers and political circles in the early nineteen fifties.

Sartre could not afford to be as direct as Aristophanes: no character is given the name of a well-known journalist or politician. But there are numerous and precise ties with the contemporary situation. Current slogans are caricatured. *Soir à Paris* is fictitious, but its competitors, *France Soir* and *Paris Presse,* are not. Names of persons who were well-known at the time sprinkle the dialogue: Malenkov, Khrushchev, Thierry Maulnier, McCarthy, Adenauer, Franco, Kravchenko, Herriot, Cartier, Georges Duhamel, Lazareff.

As far as significance is concerned, quick obsolescence is a price that a precisely committed piece of writing should have to pay. How many people remember the Kravchenko case? In the early nineteen fifties, before the Soviet intervention in Hungary, some French intellectuals like Sartre thought it advisable, if not to become members of the Communist Party, at least to be unrewarded fellow-travelers. Sartre tried to play the part of an anti-anticommunist. A double negation is not always the equivalent of an affirmation. Anti-anti-red may mean yellow, or violet, or gray. But if you are a dyed-in-the-wool white, or green, or red, it does not make much difference. Whoever is not with me is against me.

Revolts were quashed in Budapest, then Prague. Charles de Gaulle officially started the detente game. Defections continued. But Sartre could not dump a fellow-writer like Solzhenitsyn in the same basket as his (supposed) Kravchenko. Where are the *Nekrassovs* of yesteryear?

Did the play of Aristophanes contribute to the arrest and condemnation of Socrates? I don't know. I definitely think that Sartre's play had no effect on the cold war. Yet I cannot prove it. Neither *Nekrassov* nor Sartre's later writings, political interventions for instance, had the result of throwing Sartre-Socrates into jail. French rulers were careful not to imitate Russian rulers or Louis XV. They frustrated Sartre's attempts in this direction. Half-hearted attempts it seems.

In the play, Sartre's political preferences show mainly through Véronique, the only character who is not treated farcically, apart from Valera, who is deliberately flippant. Her allusion to Billancourt, where some Renault plants are located, to refer to industrial workers in general, is a cliché taken from French Communist language. Yet, in the context, it does not appear to be intended to make fun of Véronique.

In May 1968, some Parisian students came to realize that manual workers could not be forced into an allegory of the Worker. Good intentions are neither a sufficient, nor even a necessary, condition of good politics. I have the impression that, since the end of the latest world war, the difference between rightist and leftist tendencies in France has reduced to that between hypocrisy and self-hypocrisy. In terrorist closed worlds, the difference disappears.

Valera professes disgust for a "high Soviet dignitary who would come to Paris for the express purpose of helping the enemies of his people and his party" (p. 205). The application of the virtue of loyalty to the political domain is incongruous. Shall we say that this verbal gesture is precisely designed to illustrate Valera's personal ethics and its lack of pertinence? To say the least, the passage is not clearly ironical.

On the other hand, Sartre has avoided making his main character, Valera, undergo an edifying political conversion. Valera's decision to help Véronique's friends is inspired by personal motives under special circumstances. Like Goetz in *The Devil,* Valera belongs to the category of the adventurer. But he does not go through dialectical phases like Goetz, nor is there any attempt to make his last gesture appear as a conversion: "I used to dictate to the father, I shall dictate to his daughter" (p. 284). Sartre had contrasted adventurer with militant in a short essay, *Portrait de l'Aventurier (Situations,* VI, 7-22). Did he dream of "totalizing" epic and anarchist aspirations plus dogged collectivist requirements? Would small-scale terrorism be an answer? Outside La Fontaine's fable, it is more often the blind who guide paralytics than vice-versa.

It is also to be noted that the words of another character, Demidoff, a *bona fide* defector, serve as a satire of a mentality forged by the Soviet regime. He laments the fact that he has "fallen off" history "as a little bird falls from the nest" (p. 266). Yet he drinks to the glory of the "historical process," even though it will crush him, and to the bomb which will annihilate life on earth (p. 267). In a comic mood, Demidoff's plight echoes that of Bukharin, as Sartre imagines it at the end of *Saint Genet.*

The inevitable coincidence of the end of the historical process (Lord Man's saga) with the end of the human race seems to have troubled Sartre:

> To assure me that the human species would perpetuate me, it was agreed in
> my head that it would not end. To die in its midst would be to be born and
> become infinite, but, if someone put forward the hypothesis that a

cataclysm might one day destroy the planet, even in fifty thousand years, I was horrified. Even now that I am disenchanted I cannot think without dread of the sun cooling off: it does not matter if my fellow-men forget me the day after my burial; as long as they live, I shall haunt them, elusively, nameless, present in each of them like the billions of dead men whom I do not know, yet preserve from annihilation. But, if humankind disappears, it will kill its dead for good. (*Les Mots,* p. 209)

*   *   *

The play is long, too long perhaps. This is a tendency which affects most of Sartre's writings after 1950. The plot could have dispensed with the three scenes of the first tableau, which take place by the Seine and in which the main characters are two hoboes, who will not reappear. On the other hand, these scenes are enjoyable in themselves: they allow Sartre to give free rein to his verve, insert witty rejoinders, display his sense of lively dialogue. In the second tableau, the marginal scene in which Palotin gives a cheque to the mayor of Travadja, a devastated foreign town, exploits the comic device of a bogus foreign language for its own sake. The mayor's terse words: "Navoki, Novoka, Kékoré" are translated by the interpreter as: "The children of Travadja will never forget the generosity of the French people" (p. 57). These scenes, as well as passages in other scenes, may be called padding if one adopts an austere conception of dramatic composition. But they are as enjoyable now as when *Nekrassov* was first produced, and they contribute to providing the play with a remarkable variety of characters, from hoboes to policemen to politicians and members of a board of directors.

The style of *Nekrassov* oscillates between the colloquial and the literary. In itself, this instability is a comic factor. Changes of style are not made to correspond to which character is speaking. One of the hoboes says: *Faut qu'on soye* (p. 19), which is a colloquial equivalent for "we must be." But the same character is not without poetic leanings: "The water flows, the moon does not flow" (p. 17). And the other hobo turns into a character in an elegant classical comedy by Molière when he assures Valera he had only the latter's interest in mind: *"Je le sais, Monsieur, je n'avais souci que du vôtre"* (p. 24). One of the policemen shifts from the popular *m'étonnerait* to the literary *hélas* to express doubt, then regret. On entering Sibilot's apartment, one character expresses his great liking for it and predicts that he will be sorry to leave. He also remarks philosophically that man is a strange animal, and makes an ironical toast "to the defenders of Western culture." He happens to be a police inspector.

The most memorable comic effect occurs when Valera meets the members of the board of directors. As Nekrassov, he pretends to know the names of those who will be liquidated when the Russian army occupies France. So, while the directors greet Valera-Nekrassov with the usual *Enchanté,* the latter answers with the threatening, but flattering, *Exécuté,* except in the case of the chairman, who is shocked when told *Enchanté.* The others infer immediately that, since he is not on the list, he must be a traitor.

* * *

Here and there, various characters abandon the kind of speech that would fit their role in the plot and appear to be talking for the sake of being witty or at least amusing. With Valera, this behavior ceases to be gratuitous, since he is a jester by trade. He takes pride in viewing life as a comedy, in maintaining an ironical distance. He enjoys the airiness which bothered Orestes in *The Flies:* "I flew over the human enterprise and I considered it with the detachment of an artist" (p. 29).

He is conscious of his tie with the established order: like the honest Sibilot, he respects private property, since he lives off it (p. 115). And yet, he is bothered when Véronique tells him that, instead of robbing the rich, he is their ally and even their employee (p. 207). And he is shocked when he learns that, because of him, a "widow with a sick daughter" has lost her typing job with *Soir à Paris* (p. 194).

Valera is Sartre's character who is most reminiscent of Arsène Lupin, a flippant crook of genius, a master at disguise and impersonation, whose adventures, as we are told in *The Words,* Sartre used to read with delight when he was a child. In one of these adventures, written by Maurice Leblanc, Lupin, who, of course, steals only from the rich, expresses, in an ironical fashion, his respect for the social and economic order: "I am a conservative at heart, I have the same instincts as a small stock-holder, I respect tradition and authority" (*Les Aventures d'Arsène Lupin,* III, 577).

* * *

Comedies, farcical comedies, are the kind of plays I prefer. I wish Sartre had given freer rein to his considerable comic talents in his theatre. And I wish *Nekrassov* were more homogeneously farcical.

Véronique is less of a bore than Hilda in *The Devil.* But she is still a blot on the landscape. Asking someone to repeat, she resorts to the stilted *Plaît-il* (p. 281). This is far from enough to caricature her verbal gestures. She seems to have the vague ambition of becoming a Giraudoux heroine. Too late. Valera is also made to stand apart from the other characters. Both Véronique and he are allowed a pedestal. Such a lack of balance is not special to *Nekrassov*. I could say the same for most comedies I read.

Gestures can be ridiculous if they display an incongruity between means and goal, or between intentions and results. Motley gestures: not a personified individual as a whole. Otherwise, we would veer toward uneasy pity, or nasty laughter. In order to avoid these shifts, all characters in a comedy should appear as characters of comedians. They must be detached as ludic roles from gestures as ludicrous.

This can be done by having witty, ironical, humorous characters. Their verbal gestures are not ludicrous, they point to gestures that would be ludicrous. These ludicrous gestures are not enacted, or, if they are, the characters double them with irony directed at their own behavior. So we smile or laugh with the characters, not at them.

Another strategy consists in presenting characters as clowns rather than wits. The characters in this case are still comedians. But the way they play (and the way the actors should play) does not reveal an intention to make fun of gestures they do not enact, nor of gestures they enact. I cannot attribute to such characters an intention to be witty. And yet I cannot reduce them to their ludicrous gestures. Their detachment is like a transparent margin; they are blank characters.

To speak in Sartrean terms, they illustrate the transcendence of nothingness without committing it as project. To speak in Bergsonian terms, their behavior may appear mechanical because devoid of personal intentions. But the ludicrous gestures are not reduced to mechanisms. They have a life of their own, supported by the characters as enigmatic mouthpieces. Some of the plays which will be mentioned in the conclusion can provide examples.

Can this strategy be adopted in the soliloquizing aspect of an essay?

ALTONA (1959)

Les Séquestrés d'Altona (here *Altona*) takes place (legendarily) in the house of the Gerlach family, in contemporary Germany: the father, who owns shipyards, his daughter Leni, his son Werner, who is married to Johanna, a former actress, and another son, Frantz, who is officially dead and who has not left his room for thirteen years (since 1946). Only Leni communicates with him. The father has cancer. He would like to see Frantz again. The latter has so far refused to see him.

In his room, Frantz spends his time playing again and again the part of Defense Attorney for Mankind. He records his words on tape, pretends to be speaking to the judges, "the Crabs," whom he imagines as the successors of mankind on earth. They can reconstitute past events, but cannot understand and judge by themselves. Frantz also pretends to believe that Germany is still as it was at the end of the second world war, or worse. Leni plays up to him. But Johanna, who wants to free her husband from the obligation to remain in the house after the father's death, manages to talk to Frantz. She is intrigued by his game; but, with her, Frantz can no longer pretend that it is not a game. And Leni, who loves her brother incestuously and resents Johanna's visits, finally destroys the fiction that Germany, according to Frantz's wishes, has been slowly and dutifully dying during all these years, by bringing a newspaper which features an article about the postwar recovery of the Gerlach shipyards. Frantz leaves the room where he had confined himself, drives away with his father on a suicide run. Leni takes his place in the room. Frantz's voice, speaking to the Crabs, is heard on the tape recorder.

*   *   *

In *Altona*, reflexivity is once more in evidence. Frantz's room (acts II and IV) is a stage within the stage (the house, acts I and III). Act V mixes the two: Frantz comes out of his room; Leni takes his place; outside the room, the tape recorder repeats an address of Frantz to the Crabs.

Frantz has enclosed himself in a theatrical cave. His endless defense of humankind is pure gestures: it has no utilitarian purpose within the play. His room is likened to "Hell." The way it is described in the stage directions may remind one of the attic in *Dead without Burial*. One may also recall Garcin in *No Exit*. Like Garcin, he is interested in playing the game of self-justification endlessly. But, unlike Garcin, he chose his theatrical stage. And he chose imaginary Crabs (also a compliant sister) as partners-opponents. Furthermore, he has diluted an attempt to justify himself in an attempt to justify allegorical figures (Man, Germany).

Despite the fascination he exerts upon them (there's no accounting for tastes), the two female characters, Leni and Johanna, react against his mania. Thus, Leni, apropos of the Crabs: "Tell them: 'You are not my judges!' and you will have nobody to fear. Neither in this world nor in the next" (p. 147). But the tribunal of the Crabs, like the silent God of Goetz, is what Frantz needs in his role of defender of man, or of a Germany that he fancies still being punished. He will acknowledge his tactic: "I wished for the death of my country, and I confined myself in order not to witness its resurrection" (p. 354).

When, like Goetz, he has grown weary of his game, he asks Johanna to assume the role of the Crabs: "I deny their competence, I take the case away from them and give it to you. Judge me" (p. 283). She refuses: "You don't judge those you love" (p. 286).

His father also refuses. With imperial (and vacuous) generosity, he takes upon himself the responsibility for everything Frantz did. Frantz is dead tired; he accepts the formula: "You will have been my cause and destiny to the end" (p. 374). The father too is tired. He has the impression of having been reduced to a figurehead in a firm he owns, but no longer manages. He turns the firm into an allegorical figure which is conveniently supposed to have forced Frantz to retreat from utilitarian activities to theatrical gesturing: "To act, you took the greatest risks and, you see, it (in French "she") transformed all your acts into gestures" (p. 369). So the two characters are reconciled. As in the gospel of John, the father and the son can even be one, but in death, according to Frantz: "As long as we live, we shall be two" (p. 372). Denouement, *analusis*: dissolution. No last judgment, no condemnation or redemption. Entropy. In *The Flies,* Orestes was one with the Holy Ghost, dismissed father Jupiter, and fled the Argives. He still had space, and energy to dissipate. To waste?

Altona contains dramatized evocations of Frantz's past. But, unlike *Dirty Hands, Altona* avoids turning them into one long inner play. An abrupt interaction between present and past occurs when Frantz, who is talking to Johanna in his room about Klages, one of the characters in the recalled scenes, says: "Klages wished for our defeat," and when Klages, not Johanna, answers within the recalled scene: "I do not wish for that; I want it" (p. 307).

This is not all. It appears later that the recalled scene was cooked up by Frantz, apparently to pretend to Johanna that he never tortured any prisoner during the war on the Russian front. That Frantz did torture prisoners is a narrative axiom which Sartre takes care to confirm with the testimony of the father. On the other hand, the misleading scene may be received, after the fact, as showing that, after so many years, so much brooding and play-acting, Frantz's memories have lost a true-or-false status and have veered to the neither-true-nor-false status of fiction. Frantz is pleased to entertain more or less unpleasant dreams about his past.

Evocations of past events are not concentrated at the beginning of the play. Revelations are gradual and discontinuous. In my judgment, *Altona* is too long, especially the first act, overburdened with information the dramatist has to slip to spectators or readers. But there are interconnected suspenses: regarding Frantz's past (to be finally made clear by Leni), the present (Germany's new prosperity, with which Frantz is to be confronted), the future (whether Frantz will be engulfed in imbecillity, or abandon his game and come out of his room, and with what result).

At the end of *Altona,* the tape recorder has the last word. An appropriate choice, in view of the content of the verbal gestures taken over by the machine:

> The age would have been good if man had not been hunted by his cruel immemorial enemy, the carnivorous species that swore to get rid of him, the hairless and nasty beast, man. One and one is one, this is our mystery . . . . Perhaps there will be no centuries after ours. Perhaps a bomb will have snuffed out the lights. Everything will be dead: the eyes, the judges, time. Night. O tribunal of night, you who were, who will be, who are, I have been! I have been! I, Frantz von Gerlach, here, in this room, I put the age on my shoulders and I said: I shall answer for it.

In *Un Coup de Dés, Mallarmé,* recently echoed by Lévi-Strauss at the end of his *Mythologiques,* wrote more radically: "Nothing will have taken place but the place . . . Except perhaps for a constellation" (*Oeuvres Complètes,* pp. 474-477). Sartre prefers conflicts of anthromorphic characters to arrangements of stars, or stones; he privileges a dramatic type of understanding. At least, at last, he consents to have a speaking machine replace "men, madmen." As far as I am concerned, the indifference of the toy has a greater derisive power than the sarcasms Frantz himself sometimes added to his grandiloquent gestures. The machine, which is neither a human nor nonhuman animal, delivers schizophrenic talk about the human: allegorized value and allegorized species. The plaything addresses nobody, not even itself. It has recorded the past for no interpreter. Of course, the spectators, in their ludic field, overhear it. At the end of his last original play, Sartre offers a good example of how props can be integrated in a dramatic dialectic, a possibility which is left out in his theorizing.

* * *

Being and Nothingness leaves no room for malfunctions of brains.

"Human reality" does not possess a brain (is not possessed by a brain). *Being and Nothingness* leaves no room for imbecillity, madness, not even for sleep and fainting fits. It provides only for self-hypocrisy.

No doubt, it is not the business of a philosopher to talk about brains. But, at least, instead of the dualistic ("ambiguous") schema proposed in *Being and Nothingness,* one could adopt a pluralistic model of consciousness. Intersecting perspectives (or egos), more or less compatible and at odds, dispersed and concentrated, would allow for non-intersecting (unconscious) zones, imbecillitity, madnesses, more easily. If "unconscious" is meaningless, what does "conscious" mean?

Futhermore, there is no need to use the word "human" to christen a philosophical notion. It is not the kind of nickname that can fit a concept. What is the opposite of "human"? "Horsy," "fishy," "stony"? Man and Nature are allegorical figures. If we say "human-inhuman" to name a concept of value and antivalue, how are other similar concepts named? If there are none, "human-inhuman" is superfluous. It could only serve the purpose of confusing types of values.

I have already quoted a passage of *The Words* in which Sartre equates "men" with "madmen," and decides that what is said about them is neither true nor false. He means psychological assumptions and explanations, not anatomical descriptions and physiological laws, for instance bearing on central nervous systems. Sometimes, though not always, Sartre uses the term "understanding" (*comprendre*) for the former, and avoids the term "knowing" (*savoir*).

I agree. To the extent that psychology has not been reduced to physiology, it remains philosophical. And philosophy is not a cognitive activity. It does rely on many cognitive assumptions, or prejudices; it may be metacognitive; but it solves no cognitive problems. A concept of truth-falsehood can be neither true nor false.

To compose my Sartre, I summarize verbal information, extract some passages that I privilege, sweep the rest under the rug. Someone else may compose a different portrait, using other information, summarizing differently, adopting a different theoretical schema, or even the same one. Thus there would be different Sartres, but no contradictions of the type: "It is raining," "it is not raining." There can be contradictions within one essay or novel; but there can be none between two essays or pieces of fiction as such. Sartre himself, as he shows in *The Words,* was in no privileged position to decide what was I do not know what "truth" about himself.

A psychoanalytic doxa may comfort one with an impression of shared opinions. But what is thus adopted in common cannot be checked with experimental tools (that alone is objectivity). Since we remain in a realm of words, each interpreter has to make the fuzzy doxa his own if he wants to achieve some ludic integrity.

How can one try to play fair under these conditions? By complementing self-granted rights with assorted duties, a reciprocity which is often forgotten when artistic activities, i.e. games with no preestablished rules, are glorified. Making clear the chosen conceptual schema is one condition.

Being and Nothingness offers self-hypocrisy as a sort of madness. In this respect, all men would be more or less mad. But to what extent is there an awareness of self-hypocrisy, a shift from self-hypocrisy to hypocrisy, from utilitarian hypocrisy to playful comedy? It is such questions that make Sartre decide that talk "about men, about madmen," had better be received as neither true nor false. As Kean says: "I play, I don't play. I don't know." And yet, forgetting himself, Sartre will speak of "knowledge" to decorate his analysis of Flaubert.

In *The Room* (*La Chambre*), included in the collection of short stories *Le Mur,* one of the characters has shut himself up in a room. He talks as if he had hallucinations, in a cohesive way. These hallucinations are thus made to look as if they constituted a world. Since this is a story, Sartre could have imposed narrative axioms that would have made it clear whether the character was possessed or play-acting. Wisely I think, he avoids that. He gives us only the points of view of other characters: the wife and the father-in-law. The wife oscillates between one interpretation and the other. Her attitude is similar to that of Leni and Johanna in *Altona.* There is no denouement in the short story. In *Altona,* it is the antagonism between the two women, on which the father banked, that prevents them from acting as a chorus of accomplices and forces Frantz out of his room. Out of his imperfectly closed world.

As dramatist, Sartre cannot give us narrative axioms decreeing whether Frantz is play-acting or possessed. But he gives us much more information than in *The Room.* Frantz says much more than the character in the short story; and Sartre takes advantage of stage directions bearing on how Frantz's verbal gestures should be enacted. The dramatized evocations of the past may suggest hallucinations; but the evidence in favor of play-acting is too strong to allow a docile acceptance of possession.

For instance, it is a postulate of Frantz's world that Germany is still being punished, that Germans are still massacred, or starving. But his room and his body cannot be completely cut off from their utilitarian surroundings in an historical Germany. He has to eat, drink, and be left in peace. He eats oysters and drinks champagne. These choices fit the Crabs and bubbly eloquence. But they do not fit the postulate, which should equally apply to the Gerlach family.

One might also raise the question of the servants. The Gerlach household must have servants. Indeed, they are mentioned in *Altona*. But Sartre has (dubiously) managed to dismiss them from the stage, so as to allow Leni to function as buffer more easily (for thirteen years!).

In French, it is sometimes said of some people that they know everything and understand nothing. In *Altona,* the Crabs are supposed to be such divine computers. Understanding demands empathy, i.e. antipathy and sympathy. But comprehension does not yield objectively testable propositions. Frantz tries to make his crabs understand in a certain way, that is to say, to persuade himself. But, so doing, he can only improvise and rehash a drama with a double character.

In my terms, self-hypocrisy may be interpreted as an attempt to legendize oneself: ludic and utilitarian goals are confused. Sartre suggests how allegory can be added to legend. He postulates (in theory) that each human continuously tries (and fails) to "totalize" himself. Each human would have to include others in his perspective. So, in order to totalize himself, he would have to try to absorb others. This attempt might be said to constitute a Sartrean kind of madness, or hybris.

I adopt the postulate that, in order to personify himself, someone has to personify something else as enemy or opponent: allies and partners are insufficient. The last human on earth may have to personify the sun as Phoebus and the moon as Artemis. But I do not adopt the postulate that each human tries at all times to totalize himself. I should rather assume that some packs of neurones manage to neutralize others.

Actually, the Sartrean principle that to be human is to choose and be forced to choose appears at odds with a project of self-totalization. To choose is to reject. One might try to absorb rejection in a Hegelian manner: what is rejected would somehow be conserved, transfigured. But it may simply be killed. Or, if it is not killed, it may go on living a parallel life of its own, without being digested by, or entering into dramatic conflict with, what has been chosen.

Another thing. Sartre says that a person has to solve his problems, his dramatic conflicts, or explode. It may be objected that many, though not all, problems of daily life are not like mathematical problems or tight dramatic conflicts. They are not solved; they dissolve. You brood over the terms of a problem, find a solution. But the terms of the problem are no longer there. So you have solved today yesterday's problem. Instead of conflicts and solutions, anachronistic incongruities. A synchronic assemblage may be pictured as made of intertwined threads of various colors, some ending, some starting, others continuing. If the process is historical, not fictional, don't ask for a nice tapestry.

Some of Sartre's characters in his narrative and dramatic fiction do not echo his theorizing. I am thinking in particular of the illiterate shepherd in *Roads of Freedom.* Other characters echo Sartre's metadramatic conception of human existence (Hugo, Kean); some may be interested in a kind of self-totalization (Garcin). In *Altona,* Frantz adds to these traits an attempt to identify himself with the allegorical figure of Man (like Orestes and Goetz).

Family stories bore me. The glue on kinship labels has a musty smell. In part, *Altona* is a family drama. Outside the tape recorder, my main interest lies in the connections between the play-acting Frantz and Sartre in his ludic writing role. Those are not family relationships.

*   *   *

Torture is evoked in *Altona,* but not in the direct and relentless manner noted in *Dead without Burial.* Is it supposed to help motivate Frantz's behavior nicely? It may instead be considered a false scent.

Sartre was probably thinking of torture in the Algerian war, as practiced at least on the French side. In 1958, Henri Alleg managed to publish his testimony on such happenings in *La Question.* Sartre wrote an article about it. Straight, candid propaganda (I attach no *a priori* derogatory tinge to this word). The unsold copies of the weekly in which Sartre's article had appeared were seized. Thus the French government added to the publicity. It was already widely known or surmised that torture was practiced in the Algerian war. But making a splash is far from superfluous. It may be assumed that, added to Alleg's book, Sartre's article contributed to the lassitude of French politicians, hence to the return of Charles de Gaulle. But that was not what Sartre said he wanted. So, as in the case of *Dirty Hands,* he may have thought that his writing had been politically effective in a way he did not like. Dramatic irony.

In his article about Alleg's book, Sartre assumes that the intention of torturers is to "tame the most obscene, ferocious, and cowardly beast, the human beast" (*Situations,* V, 77). But Alleg has succeeded in "reducing these tactics to their pitiful truth: they are comedies played by fools" (*Ibid.*). If Alleg did manage this comic conversion, good for him.

However, Sartre adds this interpretation of torturers: "The hatred of man they display expresses racism. For it is undoubtedly man that they want to destroy" (*Ibid.* 86). Apparently, this is the awful part. Why don't they reserve their talents for nonhuman animals?

Whether some torturers are concerned with an allegorical Man or not, I shall not try to decide. All I can say is that there is a contradiction in an attempt to destroy the allegory of Man, while torturing only some human (or nonhuman) animals.

Sartre's interpretation may be said to point out this contradiction. But there is another contradiction, which he does not point out, and seems to endorse. How can you attempt to reduce some humans to the status of an animal species among others, reserving the allegory of Man for yourself, by trying to make them, not just scream and wail, but talk in a purely human tongue?

Sartre appears to be bothered by interhuman racism, not by human racism. The article manifests a schizophrenic notion of the human. On the one hand, a divine allegorical figure; on the other, an animal species, also allegorized ("beast" in the singular). In *Of Rats and Men* and in *The Words,* he himself points to the ideological trouble. Also in *Altona,* his last original play.

(When I speak of Sartre's human chauvinism, or racism, I refer to a writing Sartre, not to a daily Sartre. As far as I know, he tortured only words with words, the word *homme* in particular, which had already been abundantly flayed and quartered anyway. You cannot deduce practical behavior from ideology, by adopting either similarity or contrast as a systematic relation between the two. Speaking of love, some Christians have tortured. But they did not invent torture. Unique gods still serve as rhetorical drugs in hot wars. But you can use other verbal drugs. You can use music too.)

The choice of crabs to represent the successors of humans on earth may be given a biographical origin: "When I was thirty-two, I had some very unpleasant hallucinations featuring crabs. Since that time, I have always considered them the symbols of the nonhuman" (*Un Théâtre de Situations,* p. 155). However, Sartre does not seem to have imagined a nonhuman posterity which might be interested in judging humans.

The choice of crabs as judges in the play combines two ideas: on the one hand, the realization that the human species, like all other species, is mortal, which is something Sartre says he does not relish, in a passage of *The Words* that has already been quoted; on the other, the idea that posterity, human this time, will be in such a different situation that it will not understand us: "What is important is to know that we shall be judged, and on the basis of criteria which are not our own. This is what is horrible" *(Un Théâtre de Situations,* p. 155). Outside of Sartre himself, to whom does "we" refer? Apparently an allegorized period.

I am left with the impression that, from Sartre's standpoint, it would be even more "horrible" if the next ages contained nobody that would be interested in writing historiography and pronouncing moral judgments on dead people. The link which permits Sartre to dream of one humankind would be cut.

When he finally stops playing his game, Frantz is still bothered by the idea that he may not be judged at all: "What becomes of me, without a tribunal?" (p. 285). He agrees to turn ulterior crabs into men: "They will be men" (p. 283). He even completes the switch: "I, the Crab" (p. 282). This transforma- tion should please a disciple of Lévi-Strauss. It echoes *Of Rats and Men,* in which "Man" is kept as a label for an allegorized ideal, while "rats" is substituted for "men," as far the members of a biological species are concerned.

In *The Words,* Sartre suggests that what is said about men (hence himself) had better be given the neither-true-nor-false status of fiction. He also cautions against "retrospective illusion." All the same, he decides to attribute to himself a precocious decision to be a writer and, so doing, to "protect the human species" (*Les Mots,* p. 144). Without having received this mandate from anyone.

In *Altona,* Frantz play-acts as the self-appointed defender of the human race (and Germany). Also as its only witness. When he becomes weary of his game, he says:

The witness of Man . . . (*Laughing.*) And who could that be? Of course, Madam, it is Man, a child would guess that. I confess there is a vicious circle.

(*With somber pride.*) I am Man, Johanna; I am every man and the whole
Man, I am the Age (*sudden farcical humility*), like anybody (p. 284).

In *The Words,* Sartre still insists that each man is the whole Man
(without stage directions). Picture Platonic Ideas of Man walking the streets in
throngs, and calling each other pale imitations, forgeries. Unless they take the
precaution of isolating themselves in rooms, with nourishing sisters, in order to
write or dictate to tape recorders. Without trying to publish, preferably.

In *Altona,* the father says this about Frantz: "When you do nothing, you
believe you are responsible for everything" (p. 79). He mocks the theoretical
principle, laid down in *Being and Nothingness,* that each human is responsible
for "the world," since he agrees to live in it (and since the historical field is
theoretically one). I have already suggested this application of the principle: if
you believe you are responsible for everything, you can do nothing. Or you are
responsible for nothing in particular.

Frantz answers affirmatively when Johanna asks him: "So everybody
does the opposite of what he wants?" (p. 281). This is a generalization of what
Sartre, in an interview, chose to say about himself as a writer. He would have
written "exactly the contrary" of what he wanted to write. This conception of
dramatic dialectic is too convenient. If you believe dramatic irony is so strict,
all you have to do is write in a Machiavellian way: the contrary of what you
feel inclined to write. Which reminds me that Marx was an *agent provocateur*
for a capitalist cause. "Objectively."

In *The Words,* discarding freedom and responsibility for an impression
of dramatic coherence, Sartre concludes his analysis of his childhood with
these words: "Thus my destiny was forged" (*Les Mots,* p. 138). And I have
already quoted the passage in a 1960 interview where Sartre decides that,
since his youth, he has experienced "total powerlessness." In *Altona,* a tired
Frantz accepts without protest his father's suggestion that he was condemned
to futile play-acting. I have already likened Jupiter in *The Flies* to the sketch
Sartre draws of his grandfather in *The Words.* Regarding Frantz's father, I had
better leave Sartre's grandfather alone.

In his secluded room, Frantz says to Leni: "I am writing history and you
come to disturb me with your anecdotes" (p. 133). Later: "History is a sacred
speech" (p. 138). Later: "You will all be acquitted. Even you: it will be my
vengeance. I shall make History pass through a mousehole" (p. 146). History
with a capital is only a (the?) story of mankind, the epic of Lord Man. Frantz
dictates it to a tape recorder, rehashing it again and again. The tape recorder

will be content to deliver a fragment of his speeches, without anybody listening, at the end of *Altona*.

The first volume of *Critique of Dialectical Reason* was published in 1960. A second volume was announced. It was supposed to show (prove?) how all the disparate conflicts between individuals, between grouped individuals, somehow composed one tight dramatic adventure, that of Humankind, against the background of Nature. Nonhuman individuals do not count. Human individuals are the ludicrous playthings, or pathetic victims (in an Aristotelian way), of dramatic ironies: the ruses of History. Except, of course, for a (the?) Hegelian composer of the epic adventure. In his ludic role, he is not of this world.

In *Nausea,* Roquentin says that adventures occur only in books. *Nausea* may be viewed as composing the adventure of a (fictional) man who reaches a revelation of gratuitous existence. He does intend to write a book, but it is not *Nausea.*

What about a book demonstrating the necessity of the adventure of Lord Man (not men)? With words, only with words. What about the denouement? Do the Greeks fade in the distance with their ships after sacking Troy? Does Man rejoin a Penelope and an Ithaca dutifully waiting for him? Does Charlemagne return to *doulce* France after massacring the Moors? How can the adventure of Man be separated from the hazardous course of the human race, about which all that can be said with philosophical certainty is that it will die? How can one avoid a tragic, or farcical, denouement? An accidental dissolution? Old age? Besides, since this figure is invented by one writer among others, it must be a fictional character.

This was not the first time Sartre announced "to be continued" without publishing the sequel. Nor was it the last. Globally, it may be said that he did not like to be stuck, that he enjoyed "betraying" himself, as he chooses to declare in *The Words.* In the case of the second volume of *Critique,* it may also be assumed that he got disgusted with the Hegelian pretense, or pretension, and could not solve the problem of a happy ending. Instead of that, he wrote a critical analysis of himself in *The Words.* He also wrote *Altona.* (For a summary of an unpublished fragment of Critique, II, see Aronson, *Jean Paul Sartre, Philosophy in The World.*)

According to Sartre, literature should be "everything" (to a writer). It could be everything if you wrote as Man talking about Man. But you can only play the role of an allegorical figure called Man. In his room, Frantz has made a total choice of himself as dramatist-director-actor (except that the eats oysters and drinks champagne). Frantz abandons his game and kills himself. Sartre does not publish his announced *Légende des Siècles,* and stops writing dramas, ten years after stopping writing narrative fiction. The relevance of *Altona*, thus presented, reduces to a kind of reflexivity. The relevance to a contemporary situation would be that writing dramatic fiction is irrelevant. At the end, the tape recorder speaks to nobody, not even itself.

Ideologically, *Altona* is the most interesting play with *The Flies* and *The Devil.* (I use the term "ideologically" with Sartre's permission, since, in *Critique,* he calls himself an ideologist, in opposition to Marx, who is supposed to be a "philosopher"; a few pages later, Sartre has forgotten his convention, calling Unamuno a philosopher.) *The Flies* echoes *Being and Nothingness* and *Existentialism is a Humanism; The Devil* echoes *Saint Genet; Altona* echoes the absence of the second volume of *Critique.* Orestes turns his singular experience into a myth of freedom, speaks as Man to Jupiter, escapes "his" men under cover of a verbal smokescreen. To allegorize himself as Man, Goetz sets up a silent God. Finally, he eliminates allegories, joins the peasant army, but the circumstances are such that he appears to be reduced to a show of solidarity. Frantz plays Man in his secluded room to an audience of silent Crabs, then kills himself. As if, outside setting up and playing allegorical figures, there was nothing to be done. At least as a dramatist, actor, dramatic character.

Sartre continued to write and publish. A lively, witty critical essay about himself (*The Words*), where he chooses to echo *Altona,* but in a lighter vein, and without forcing himself into dialectical stages like Genet. Instead of the second volume of *Critique,* which was to compose History, he wrote an immense composition of Flaubert. He chose a nineteenth-century writer as partner and opponent. I wish he had finished his book on Mallarmé, undertaken in the fifties. Mallarmé could be a more resourceful opponent than Flaubert. Deeper.

There are nineteenth-century echoes in Sartre's conception and practice of literature, echoes of a Hugolian or Hegelian Romanticism, a remake of the allegorical figure of the Writer (Thinker, Poet, Artist) as the antibourgeois bourgeois, in response to nostalgic dreams about the French Revolution and the *philosophes.* Scientific writing is not discussed in *What is Literature?.* It was less disquieting to talk about the bourgeoisie and to try to "safeguard" literature against the internal dissolution threatened by Dada. It is scientific writings that can best be presented as a "totality," as "unveiling the world," and as effectively utilitarian through technology. Sartre tries to exorcize the ghost of Dada; the more threatening ghost of science is ignored.

He did not finish the book on Flaubert. He was not as lucky as Proust, who managed to die before polishing his fat *summa.* I read that Sartre practically lost his eyesight. Being freed from the tyranny of the human face, from the sorcery of the glance, must not have been much of a relief to him. The sight of words magically coming out of a hand scratching paper must have been sorely missed.

*   *   *

Dreamily, Stendhal relied on posterity. *Altona* presents the dream of posterity as obsolete. Either posterity will not understand "us" or it will not bother about us at all. Assuming there is a human posterity. This should not trouble someone who is bent on writing for a limited contemporary audience. But what if you have the impression of being irrelevant and immaterial to such an audience?

Does the death of a reading posterity worry anybody, apart from a few *littérateurs?* The significance of *Altona* can be stretched further. The tape recorder at the end mentions a bomb that would destroy the human race (and others). While playwrights, novelists, philosophers, poets play, scientists and engineers produce ultimate weapons. This consideration seems to be of concern to more people than a few writers, though I doubt that it affects in the least Amazonian Indians, Eskimos, Bushmen in the Kalahari. This list could be lengthened.

The apocalyptic theme of ultimate weapons occurs only in snatches of *Nekrassov* and *Altona,* among Sartre's plays. Apparently, he did not see how to deal with the theme dramatically. And his uneasiness must not have been confined to his role as dramatist. Finally, he retreated to a legendary nineteenth century haunted by a legendary revolution. There was no talk of ultimate weapons then. His thoughts on the topic are most fully formulated in an article he wrote after the explosion of the first atomic bomb:

> In the next war, the earth may explode. This absurd ending would leave forever in suspense the problems with which we have been concerned for ten thousand years. Nobody would even know whether man had been able to get rid of racial hatreds, find a solution to class struggles. When you think about it, everything seems vain. And yet humankind (*feminine in French*) had one day to be given the means of its death . . . After the death of God, the death of man is announced. Henceforward, my freedom is purer: this act which I undertake today, neither God nor man will be its perpetual witness. This very day and in

eternity, I must be my own witness. Moral because I want to be so on this mined earth. And humankind as a whole, if it continues to live, will not simply live because it was born, but because it will have decided to prolong its life. No longer is there a *human species.* The community that has made itself (*herself*) the guardian of the atomic bomb is above the natural realm, because it is responsible for its life and death. You will object that we are at the mercy of a madman. It is not true: the atomic bomb is not at the disposal of just any madman. He would have to be a Hitler, and all of us would be responsible for this new Fuehrer. (*Situations,* III, 68-69)

Each of us had better tend his own garden (and stop allegorizing?). But ultimate weapons show that our gardens extend to the whole world. I ask: how can this total responsibility be put into practice? How did Sartre apply it in his dramas? Cannot the ultimate war start accidentally? What about dramatic ironies? Finally, is not each man a madman?

As author of *Being and Nothingness,* Sartre can only welcome ultimate weapons: each of us is responsible for the whole world; the human race has finally made it clear it was not an animal species. Nonhuman animals are just things anyway. How could a self-respecting dramatist devise roles for them? How could they buy books or book theatre seats?

The trouble is that the principles of *Being and Nothingness* can apply only to allegorical figures. In the quoted passages, there is a ten thousand years old "we." Philosophically, I cannot exclude the hypothesis of reincarnations. But cannot someone reincarnate a portion of a cat or dinosaur as well as a portion of one or several anthropomorphic compositions of atomic spooks? Anyhow, Sartre does not seem to be talking about reincarnations. His "we" is an allegorical projection of his personal concerns, or of concerns he deems it proper to air.

Enter two other allegorical figures, or rather two other nicknames for the same one: "humankind," "the community." Actually, "man" had already entered the stage. Very well, let us accept allegorical humankind. How can humankind prove it is above the animal realm? By killing itself of course. Otherwise, ultimate weapons would be a mere diplomatic bogeyman. But to whom would humankind prove it is above the animal kingdom? Any crabs left? I have been told radiation bombs would respect tape recorders and libraries with the complete writings of Sartre.

From the postulates embedded in the quoted passages, I extract two. The first one is that there must be one, and only one, humankind, linked by talk and judgments. In a note for the treatise of ethics which was not published, Sartre wrote: "Always the illusion of *one* humankind" (*Obliques* 18-19, p. 255). No doubt, technological progress has unified life on earth: ultimate weapons, depletion of resources, overpopulation thanks to medicine, pollution. But it has not made lives, human lives in particular, uniform. And it has not brought together humans responsibly. Maybe after next war, if it kills enough. Discriminately?

The second postulate is that the anthropomorphic type of life must be prolonged indefinitely at all costs. As if dying sooner were always worse than dying later. Sartre likes goals, is bothered by results. He prefers starts to endings. He does not publish announced sequels. Thus endings remain indefinite.

I propose this scenario (for fiction). A scientist, call him Strangelove, has at his disposal the means of bringing to quick and painless death all life forms on earth. He has drawn the spark of his moral, not technical, inspiration from, say, a line in some obscure Albigensian poet (not *Mein Kampf,* not the plays of a supposedly committed writer like Sartre). He is not interested in letting race and class struggles run their suspensefully dramatic and excitingly epic course. He simply decides that all forms of life had better disappear from the planet at once, because horrible suffering is not redeemed by anything. He does not adopt the attitude of a Leibnizian banker. Add as spice that he (or she) considers himself the chosen representative of humankind, whose mission is to rectify, not redeem, the atrocious blunders of the Platonic Engineer or biblical God. The only solution is no life at all.

Inspired like Orestes, he invents his own way. He assumes his total responsibility for the world. As a madman? We are mad in each other's eyes.

Another scenario. A scientist has invented the means of creating conscious organisms not exposed to pain, and eliminating others. So he eliminates all present life forms (including himself). The individuals he has created are pure players. Whether they are clothed in anthropomorphic garb or not does not matter. They do not consider themselves human. They do not care a rap about historiography, let alone pronouncing moral judgments on dead humans. How could they? They have no language into which to translate the words "human" and "moral." They have no marshy word language. In their games, libraries and tape recorders cannot serve as toys.

I can vaguely imagine such beings, or nonbeings. But I cannot think them philosophically. I distinguish ludic and esthetic goals from cognitive and moral goals, the historical domain from fictional or intemporal domains. I distinguish them, but cannot think them apart. Structurally, they have to be articulated; they depend on one another. Rain, fog, night are lovable. But when a pure poem is written through someone, not when someone writes an essay.

THE TROJAN WOMEN (1965)

In the introduction to his adaptation, Sartre decides that, for Euripides, this play "was a condemnation of war in general, and of colonial expeditions in particular" (p. 6). He notes that a translation was performed during the Algerian war. In Sartre's adaptation, Europe, as the continent of colonial powers, is mentioned twice: "I shall have to live and die in Europe, which means: in Hell" (p. 31); and: "Men of Europe, you scorn Africa and Asia, and you call us barbarians, I think" (p. 81).

Unfortunately, Sartre's adaptation was first performed when France was no longer at war. And, in the Algerian war, the Europeans were the losers anyway.

Bad luck. I am sorry this second part has to end, not with the bang of *Altona,* but the whimper of *The Trojan Women.*

CONCLUSION

Technically, stylistically, Sartre's plays do not isolate themselves from those written in the nineteen thirties by French dramatists currently considered major on the literary stock exchange: Giraudoux, Anouilh, Salacrou. Cocteau could be attached only in part. Ghelderode remains quite a special case.

In the late forties and during the fifties, new playwrights changed the landscape: Adamov, Beckett, Genet, Ionesco, Tardieu, Vauthier, Vian. Add Pinget and Weingarten. They may be viewed as a constellation. Their sources are Symbolist and Surrealist rather than Romantic. Add a generous sprinkling of Pirandello and a pinch of Kafka. To draw comparisons with Sartre's practice, I shall refer to a few plays by Adamov, Beckett, Genet, Ionesco, Tardieu.

These plays dissolve fabulation. By "fabulation," I mean information given about what is taking place, took place, or will take place, offstage. Within fictionalizing brackets of course. Especially information about the past.

Fabulation provides spectators or readers with narrative axioms. In a Classical or Romantic play, invalid axioms may be adopted momentarily by one or several characters: for instance, the news that someone is dead. But this axiom will be clearly rejected before the play ends.

Fabulation may be dissolved in several ways. The dramatist refrains from giving narrative axioms. Or he airs a few, but they have no impact on the behavior of the characters, so that they may pass for gratuitous fancies. Or he makes them contradictory, without solving the contradictions.

In *Godot* (*En Attendant Godot*) by Beckett, there is one messenger, or two. There is one Godot, or none, or perhaps several. In *The Chairs* (*Les Chaises*), by Ionesco, the protagonists have a son and have no son. In *The Blacks* (*Les Nègres*), by Genet, it remains undecided whether a murder has been committed or not. In *Taranne* (*Le Professeur Taranne*), by Adamov, every statement the central character makes about himself is contradicted by others, including his identity as Professor Taranne. In *The Subway* (*Les Amants du Métro*), by Tardieu, no information is given about the characters.

During the fifties, playing havoc with narrative axioms was not limited to plays to be performed. It was extended to narrative fiction in *some* of the texts that, apparently out of "isms," reviewers simply labeled "new novels." The style of such texts may still be basically narrative; but, if the narrative axioms do not cohere, these texts do not constitute coherent narrations. So they had better be called lengthy prose poems instead of novels. They extend to long strings of words the dissolution that the label "prose poem" indicates, an internal dissolution of literary modes against which Sartre attempted to react in *What is Literature?*, as far at least as poetry and fiction, not philosophy and drama, are concerned.

But, in the case of plays, the dissolution of narrative axioms has quite a different effect. As I understand it, in accord with Sartre, dramatic, or gestural, style is not narrative. No doubt, it is usually doubled by what I called a narrative shadow: utterances as symptoms. But this does not imply that fabulation cannot be dissolved. Dramatic logic, like that of narrative fiction, is basically spatial and temporal. But the "narrative" task of describing events, states of affairs, individuals, can be left to the nonverbal elements of a performance: setting, props, noises, costumes, makeup, motions. Which is what narrative fiction cannot do. If a drama is performed, you don't have to be told, for instance, that it is character A who speaks after character B.

In *Dirty Hands* and *Altona*, Sartre has turned information about the past into enacted flashbacks. In the case of *Dirty Hands*, a spectator may still wonder at the end whether Hugo killed Hoederer out of political conviction or jealousy, or simply to obey orders. But it is axiomatic that he did kill Hoederer. More generally, in Sartre's plays, questions concerning motives, intentions, may remain unsolved. But not questions regarding physical facts or the identities of characters. The spectators are definitely told that Nekrassov is Valera. Contrast *Taranne*.

As theorist, Sartre states a preference for a theatre of situations as against a theatre of *caractères*. The characters should appear to be "pure freedoms," that is to say, to take choices without being burdened with a set personality derived from past habits and situations. But Sartre, as dramatist, does burden his main characters with a past and, in most cases, their behavior is in accord with this frozen past.

Goetz goes through abrupt metamorphoses. But he still retains an imperious pride which he shares with other Sartrean protagonists, a pride which may be called a hybris if a tendency to allegorize oneself (see also Orestes and Frantz) is taken into account. Some readers or spectators may consider that these two traits, or even the first one only, suffice to constitute a set personality. Goetz and Frantz shed their hybris at the end. They are tired;

the play must end; there must be, if not a solution, at least a dissolution. The play ends. Divested of his pride or hybris, a Sartrean protagonist has to disappear.

On the other hand, Sartre's reliance on unequivocal narrative axioms helps him to fashion tight situations from the start, and thus launch a tight dramatic dialectic of gestures and countergestures. This is what he suggests he wants. He likes the phrase "Caught like a rat," as far at least as fictional characters are concerned. It occurs in *No Exit, The Devil, Altona.*

However, these tight situations are not always "extreme situations," which present death as one branch of an inescapable alternative. At the beginning of *Nekrassov,* Valera makes a half-hearted attempt at suicide, and then thinks no more about it. There is no extreme situation in *Kean,* or *No Exit* (the characters are already "dead").

Furthermore, a spectator or reader may appraise a situation differently from a character. Frantz sees suicide as one branch of an alternative. He even gives the impression, toward the end, of seeing no other possibility. A spectator might say: "Very well, suppose he can no longer play his allegorical game; he can still obtain a false identity from his father and survive somewhere else. If he chooses to die, it must be because of his personality." A dramatist cannot block spectators and readers as he blocks his characters.

In the plays by other dramatists I have mentioned, there are no tight situations, no tight dramatic conflicts between or within characters. No unequivocal fabulation blocks the characters from the start. And no tight situations are created during the development. The characters jump from one verbal game to another, or stick to the same one. The indefinite situation does not force them to adopt one out of only two possible tactics.

Taranne may be considered an exception. In this case, it is the very lack of an unequivocal fabulation which is turned into an opportunity for a tight dialectic, though a repetitive one. The central character simply wants to assert narrative axioms about himself. Without seeming to want to do so, the others recurrently thwart his attempts and succeed in brainwashing him magnificently.

Like *The Unnamable,* by Beckett, *Taranne* is reminiscent of Descartes's first two *Meditations.* But in a different way: *The Unnamable* is a long prose poem; *Taranne* is a play to be performed. In his ludic role, Descartes enjoins "us" (himself and the readers?) to suppose we are asleep (while reading?). Adamov said the source of *Taranne* was a nightmare. However, the spectators are not supposed to pretend they are dreaming while they believe they are attending a performance of *Taranne*. Did Descartes suppose he was dreaming when he sent his *Meditations* to the printer, or when he dedicated the text to Sorbonne doctors? It may be said instead that he tried to lull them to sleep. It did not work.

The "thinking thing" which asserts its own existence in the *Meditations,* and which takes itself allegorically for "the human mind" in a secluded room haunted by an omniscient Crab called "the Evil Genius," then "God," is a philosophical role. Its existence is asserted axiomatically: obviously, since it is fictional. But a ludic role needs the support of an historical existence, from which it is detached. A dream confuses the two.

*   *   *

There is a strong reflexive aspect in several plays of Sartre. The same may be said about *Godot, The Chairs, The Subway, The Blacks, Taranne.* Yet there are contrasts within this Pirandellian similarity.

Both Genet and Sartre allow some of their characters to comment upon theatricality. But I have noted that, when Sartre gives free rein to his totalitarian horse, he is reluctant to let ludic goals detach themselves from the utilitarian domain. He dreams of an impossible synthesis between adventurer and militant, epic idealism and collectivist drudgery (plus hypocrisy). He is bothered by the impossibility of acclimatizing "work" in dramas. Within the plays themselves, the characters of *No Exit* have trouble adjusting to the purely theatrical conditions of their new domain; Hugo and Goetz want to come out of a cave of pure gestures. In the last three plays of Sartre (excepting *The Trojan Women*), we get a bit closer to Genet with the characters of Kean, Valera, and Frantz. For a self-respecting Genetian character is not bothered by the thought he is reduced to pure gestures. On the contrary, he may be bothered by the thought the gestures are not pure enough.

Pure copper is not to be found in the earth. Pure ludic and esthetic love is not to be found in daily life. Daydreams, or written fiction, are needed. In *The Blacks,* a fictional director speaks about play-acting. Dark-skinned actors (first level of fiction) put on masks to play whites (second level); and they cover their faces with shoe polish to obtain an essence of Blackness fairly equivalent to Whiteness. The theatricality of group mythology is thus exposed. In *Altona,* the two levels of fiction are not so distinct. Frantz is supposed to have tortured. In *The Blacks,* there is a murder theme. But it remains undecided whether one took place on the first level of fiction. Perhaps one is taking place in the wings.

In *Godot,* the protagonists sometimes allude to their waiting as a verbal game. Like the characters of *No Exit,* they seem to have to rehearse a nonexistent script indefinitely. But, in their case, there is no attempt to set up utilitarian alliances and enmities. They simply try not to sink into silence. At one point, they seem to try to compose a poem in common.

I can remember no allusions to play-acting in *The Subway, The Chairs, Taranne.* Yet the characters appear as clowns. They do not show that their intention is to play. The symptomatic meaning of their utterances remains a void; but the void, the margin, is there.

In *Taranne,* the episodic characters do not seem to have plotted to brainwash the central character, or play a hoax. All I can say is that the central character does seem intent on playing the role of Professor Taranne. In *The Subway,* the male protagonist fills his vocatives with names like "Beatrice" and "Juliet," while the female character is fleeing. He uses labels that have been stuck to an allegorical figure nicknamed "Woman." I cannot tell whether his intention is to be funny or flattering.

With such plays, labels like theatre of situations, or *caractères,* do not fit. Not even "theatre of characters." These plays illustrate a theatre of speech, of gestures, mainly verbal, which do not let characters take hold of them, and which do not take hold of characters, except in the case of the central character in Taranne. There are no conflicts between or within characters, not even a Sartrean conflict between an impression of being, and a desire not to be, reduced to pure gestures. The conflicts occur between elements of speech: sharp contradictions or incongruities.

Let me point out a few similarities and contrasts between *Altona* (1959) and *The Chairs* (1952), Ionesco's best play to my taste. *Altona* takes place (legendarily) in Germany, thirteen years after the end of the second world war. Where and when does *The Chairs* take place? No answer. There are sounds of waves. Should we picture an island? It is said that the male protagonist is a janitor. The setting does not look like the lodgings of a janitor. He is also said to be a sergeant and a field marshal (with the help of puns).

Altona relies on family relationships. In *The Chairs,* the two protagonists have a son and have no son. They do not quarrel about the discrepancy. Are they an old married couple? References to their ages vary fancifully. The "old" woman juggles chairs like a young furniture mover.

Like *Altona, The Chairs* includes the theme of a dead, or deaf, posterity. It is suggested that the male protagonist has a message to deliver to humankind. Is he a nineteenth-century writer? The female protagonist is even more compliant than Leni or Johanna. She arranges chairs for a reception during which the portentous message will be delivered by an "Orator" (a beloved disciple, a definitive exegete?). The guests arrive (an emperor among others). The two protagonists talk to them, confuse them. But the guests remain invisible and inaudible to the spectators (like Frantz's crabs). Are the two protagonists only pretending? No answer.

Commenting on *The Chairs,* Ionesco mentioned an impression of "ontological emptiness." Very well, but in a curiously Sartrean sense: the nothingness of pure consciousness. The guests are obviously blank characters. And the protagonists are blank too, since I cannot develop narrative axioms regarding their status and their intentions. But there is no dramatic emptiness. Far from it. There is a string of verbal and nonverbal gestures. The historically material chairs that serve as props play roles of chairs more powerfully than if the seated guests were visible.

In *Altona,* Frantz kills himself and lets the tape recorder speak in his place (to nobody). In *The Chairs,* the protagonists disappear through windows and let the Orator speak in their place (to the invisible guests). The tape recorder is not anthropomorphic. But it utters correct human words and sentences. The Orator is anthropomorphic. But he utters only disconnected words, fragments of words, incomprehensible sounds. Does he assume he is coherent, like a literary critic, philosopher, or political speaker? Or does he want to suggest that what he has to say is beyond words?

I should not say that the significance of *The Chairs* is lack of communication. The protagonists appear to communicate smoothly. The idea would rather be that you can communicate all the better the less you have to communicate. Above all, the idea would be that dramatic meaning is not cancelled by an absence of coherent narrative meaning, let alone philosophical meaning. To some extent, understanding oneself and understanding one another are incompatible. Still, there are overlaps, compromises. The historical field is made of such overlaps, warlike or not.

*   *   *

I have presented Sartre's aphorism: "Philosophy is dramatic and drama is philosophical" as a symptom of a Hegelian tendency already present in *Being and Nothingness* (1943).

Much more than in *Nausea* (1938). At the end of this philosophical novel, Roquentin vaguely hopes that the ludic role of a novelist will "save" him. But "in the past, only in the past." He thus attempts to recover partially from a revelation that experiences do not happen according to a temporal logic, or any other logic for that matter. At the end of the revelatory time out, the nausea of basic gratuitousness (which I call non-sense) is replaced by the "smile" of a "little sense." Since it does not separate what is signified from the experienced signs, this little sense may be called poetic.

Being and Nothingness narrows the perspective. Existence is reduced to the human condition and is presented as temporalizing and temporalized. So, types of meaning that do not temporalize (pure poetry, pure philosophy) are implicitly rejected, or downgraded, as opposed to a narrative and dramatic type of meaning and understanding.

Furthermore, while *Nausea* granted a special status to esthetic entities (less clearly to ludic roles), *Being and Nothingness* does not distinguish between historical and fictional time. Hence a tendency to throw esthetic contemplation, ludic activities, utilitarian activities, into the same total basket.

Finally, each "human reality" is supposed to try to totalize itself. This is an attempt to be God. Since the others are only human, it is an attempt to be Man. Romantically, God is replaced by Man, Eternity by History; also, as Sartre suggests in *The Words,* Prophet by Writer and Church by Literature. We are still dealing with allegorical figures.

Confusions between moral and ludic-esthetic values, or substitutions of the latter for the former, can be observed in quite a few writers. They are an occupational hazard. In *Nadja,* for instance, Breton pictures daily life as a sort of poetic novel with resonances between events that challenge probability. In *The Myth of Sisyphus,* Camus praises a reduction of daily life to a series of dramatic roles against the background of mortality. He prefers tragedy to farce: it is a higher genre. He takes advantage of mortality to reduce moral goals, not ludic goals, to meaninglessness.

To bring philosophy closer to drama, Sartre adds allegory to legend. However, *Being and Nothingness* presents the Hegelian project of a consciousness, not only as inevitable, but also as an illusion: it has to fail. A person will be prevented by others and his own duality (why not plurality?) from being *the* Person and absorbing the whole play. He can but play the role of Man. In his ludic role, a philosopher-dramatist can forget about the rest and identify with the particular world being composed. But not with the finished world. Even less with the published world.

Sartrean Cro-Magnons ("Big Holes"), a subspecies of an animal species also known as *Homo Sapiens,* do not have to worry about hunting and slaughtering Small Hole or No Hole animals. Steaks are readily available in Lutetia. So, on the inner wall of his skull, or Platonic cave, or haunted house, a Sartrean Cro-Magnon paints something called "Man," with which he identifies himself and hopes magically to snare other Cro-Magnons and devour them like a Hegelian ogre to fill his big hole. But, once he has finished painting, he can no longer identify with what is painted. Besides, a mess of unique Men (or Gods) is the result of various Cro-Magnons painting their own allegorical figures.

In Sartre's plays, the only characters who obviously try to identify themselves with an allegorical Man are Orestes, Goetz, Frantz. The project to be Man can count at first on a convenient Jupiter; then it turns for help to an absent God; finally, it has to resort to silent and future Crabs. Orestes manages to remain Man by fleeing the Argives and disappearing from the stage. Goetz becomes a leader of men again, but his pose as Man is shattered. Frantz clearly shows he can only play the allegorical role, and in seclusion. Like a philosopher-dramatist.

(Various spectators and readers unacquainted with Sartre's essays may have found the pseudophilosophical utterances of Orestes, Goetz, Frantz, particularly confusing. As Michel Contat presumes in *Explication des Séquestrés d'Altona,* it is probable that more people have been "exposed" to some of Sartre's plays than to other texts. But no inference regarding reactions and interpretations can be drawn from this assumption.)

If the Hegelian hybris of a Sartrean soul must fail, epic has to turn to tragedy or farce. The ending is tragic in *Altona,* though Frantz is somewhat farcical in his room. Like Frantz, Sartre stopped playing the role of dramatist Man talking about Man to men that may have been just as deaf as crabs. To my regret, he did not continue with more definite farces, better balanced than *Nekrassov.* Unless *The Words* is counted as one.

Let us play the game of motives. Why did Sartre stop writing plays? Like Frantz, he was tired of the role of dramatist. He was tired of self-allegorizing characters; and he found no other idea. As far as farce is concerned, he considered that the dramatists I mentioned had done the job. He decided that they made his dramatic technique look obsolete. He came to think that dramatic fiction, as well as narrative fiction, had proved its irrelevance. Practiced by him or others, it could not do the sort of job proposed, not very hopefully, not very precisely, in *What is Literature?*.

Did Sartre even try? The significance of his plays is not precisely and unequivocally oriented toward a contemporary situation. Except for *Nekrassov*, which was obviously ineffective. This is not a criticism, since I do not consider that fiction, poetry, or even philosophy, can have a broad utilitarian impact, at least under conditions such as those that have prevailed in France and other Western countries in the twentieth century. It is to other kinds of writings and publications that one should turn for observable utilitarian repercussions.

The other plays I mentioned do not reveal a clear utilitarian intention either. Even *The Blacks*, since this play shows that Blackness is a theatrical allegory as well as Whiteness (or Yellowness: it would have been better to substitute say, Greenness and Blueness). However, it may be alleged that these plays are more relevant to a contemporary linguistic and ideological situation than those of Sartre, except *Nekrassov* in part. For they point to a dispersion of myths into incohesive and transitory slogans that anyone, any group, can adopt and reject like synthetic socks. By itself, this situation prevents literature from coalescing into a countermyth, which is what Sartre suggested that it should do in *What is Literature?*. This sloganization has affected Parisian literary milieux. To remain an arbiter of fashion, a Petronius like Barthes had to switch terminologies, or jargons, quite often, instead of making one more rigorous, go deeper.

The dissolution of literary kinds of writing, which passed through an acute stage with Dada, has extended from poetry to novels, and then to dramas (after 1960). An appearance of religiosity is still maintained by some people. But the sacred word is no longer *littérature,* or *poésie.* For some years, it has been *écriture,* an even more conceptually meaningless password. No doubt, fairly stable novels and dramas continue to come out abundantly. But, for someone interested in new directions, they do not count.

Did Sartre even try to concoct a countermyth, an ideological "counter-mystification"? Orestes extols the myth of Man equated with Freedom. This was hardly new. In the other plays, nothing else develops. What is most persistent is the reflexive theme of humans as dramatic actors. In *Being and Nothingness*, Sartre endeavored to give an ontological basis to this traditional *moraliste* theme.

In my view, attempts to produce countermyths can but be detrimental to ludic and esthetic integrity in fiction, philosophy, poetry. Moreover, I doubt that, assuming this tactic were effective, its practical repercussions would be useful rather than baneful. Given the conditions that have obtained for some

time in Western countries, and correlatively on the planet, the dialectic of
myth and countermyth can no longer be afforded. If, beyond intrinsic
enjoyment, philosophical and literary games can be useful, it is by contributing
to distinctions and articulations between utilitarian values and those that are
not. Instead of confusing them. If play is suppressed in theory, dreams will
infect work in practice.

One might say that, to show he was equipped with a Sartrean soul, Sartre
had to write as if he were dazzled by a mirage of Man. In his essays, not just by
plaguing some of his characters with hybris. And he also had to recognize the
mirage as such. Instead of writing about History in the announced second
volume of *Critique of Dialectical Reason,* he wrote about what he calls his
"neurosis" in *The Words* (in the terminology of *Being and Nothingness*: bad
faith, self-hypocrisy). He says he has carried out to the end a "long and cruel
task" of atheism. I am not sure he finally resigned himself to equating the
allegories of Man and God. I consider Hegelian thinking, and Marxist thinking
to the extent it is Hegelian, as an attempt to restore medieval thinking, to the
extent medieval thinking is bent on allegorizing.

Sartre's totalitarian tendency may be viewed as a repercussion of the
Nazi phenomenon, his anthropomania as bolstered by a catastrophic fame.
But I had better not start wondering about a Sartre who might have been, if part
of what happened had not happened. Beware of counterfactuals.

*   *   *

In *What is Literature?,* Sartre maintains a conception of literary
activities limited to a few professionals. Other people, including reviewers, are
supposed to read, attend performances, and react as the Writer desires. In a
1960 interview, Sartre abandons some of his former positions. He adds: "But
I retain a conviction, only one, to which I shall cling: writing is a need for
everyone. It is the highest form of the need to communicate" (*Situations,* IX,
38). Lautréamont, then Breton, had already said that poetry should be written
by everyone.

I consider that compositions of fiction, philosophy, poetry, are essen-
tially ludic activities. So I can but concur. With some provisos. Nobody should
be forced to pursue such activities beyond a learning stage: the postulate that
writing games are a universal need should not be enforced. On the other hand,
everyone should be given some elementary training. An active literariness
should be added to literacy. Some official French poets appear unable to tell an
alexandrine from a centipede: they boast they cannot count. They don't have

to write alexandrines. But, if they don't, they should at least know that they don't and why. Someone who wants to learn to play soccer should not simply be told to "express" himself. Playing with and against words should be taught technically. In particular by resorting to pastiches and parodies as exercises. Thus, the shreds of religiosity which still cling to the teaching of literature could be dissolved. Pastiches would turn major and minor saints into ludic partners and opponents.

If everybody interested in literary or philosophical sport continued to write past the learning stage, would anybody read anybody? Would anybody get published? I don't know whether Sartre, who seems attached to the dream of a humankind linked by literary writing and reading, entertained these questions. Judging by the passage of the 1960 interview which has been quoted, he does not seem to realize that, if they are universalized and put into practice, the postulates of a need to write and of a need to communicate the results (to readers other than oneself and a few polite friends) are incompatible. Priests need parishioners, prophets disciples. But you do not need spectators to enjoy bicycling, playing tennis, playing with words against words. You do not need autograph hunters. Not even the fathers and mothers to whom scholarly books are dedicated.

When he speaks of the Writer, Sartre does not consider that only a small fraction of manuscripts can be published, and only a very small fraction of published manuscripts read and reread seriously by more than a few hundred people. If many more people continued to play writing games, and tried to publish, how could publishing continue to function, even as poorly as it does now? There would be no paper left for printing anyway. Nobody could even be allowed to spend his days amassing thousands of pages like Proust writing on Proust or Sartre on Flaubert. Apocalypse of the Writer. Not as revelation: the allegorical Writer has already been abundantly revealed, by Sartre and Proust among others. But, given the extinction of the prey, the correlative Reader: death.

Anthopolis, brumaire 189

BIBLIOGRAPHY

TEXTS BY SARTRE

Alexandre Dumas, Kean, adaptation de Jean-Paul Sartre. Paris: Gallimard, 1954.

Bariona, in Michel Contat and Michel Rybalka, *Les Ecrits de Sartre.* Paris: Gallimard, 1970.

Les Chemins de la Liberté, 3 vols. Paris: Gallimard, 1945-1949.

Critique de la Raison Dialectique. Paris: Gallimard, 1960.

Le Diable et le Bon Dieu. Livre de Poche Collection. Paris: Gallimard, n.d.

L'Etre et le Néant. Paris: Gallimard, 1943.

Euripide, Les Troyennes, adaptation de Jean-Paul Sartre. Paris: Gallimard, 1965.

L'Existentialisme est un Humanisme. Paris: Nagel, 1946.

Huis Clos, suivi de Les Mouches. Folio collection. Paris: Gallimard, n.d.

L'Imaginaire. Paris: Gallimard, 1940.

Les Mains Sales. Livre de Poche collection. Paris: Gallimard, n.d.

Les Mots. Folio collection. Paris: Gallimard, n.d.

Le Mur. Paris: Gallimard, 1939.

La Nausée. Paris: Gallimard, 1938.

Nekrassov. Folio collection. Paris: Gallimard, n.d.

La P . . . Respectueuse, suivi de Morts sans Sépulture. Folio collection. Paris: Gallimard, n.d.

Saint Genet Comédien et Martyr. Paris: Gallimard, 1952.

Les Séquestrés d'Altona. Livre de Poche collection. Paris: Gallimard, n.d.

Situations, I. Paris: Gallimard, 1947.

Situations, II. Paris: Gallimard, 1948.

Situations, III. Paris: Gallimard, 1949.

Situations, IV. Paris: Gallimard, 1964.

Situations, V. Paris: Gallimard, 1964.

Situations, VI. Paris: Gallimard, 1964.

Situations, IX. Paris. Gallimard, 1972.

Un Théâtre de Situations. Idées collection. Paris: Gallimard, 1973.

TRANSLATIONS OF SARTRE'S TEXTS (not guaranteed)

Being and Nothingness, tr. Hazel Barnes. New York: Philosophical Library, 1956.

The Condemned of Altona, tr. Sylvia and George Leeson. New York: Knopf, 1961.

The Devil and the Good Lord, and two other plays (Kean, Nekrassov), tr. Sylvia and George Leeson. New York: Knopf, 1960.

Existentialism, tr. Bernard Frechtman. New York: Philosophical Library, 1947.

Imagination, a Psychological Critique, tr. Forrest Williams. Ann Arbor: University of Michigan Press, 1962.

Kean, tr. Frank Hauser. London: Davis-Poynter, 1972.

Kean, or Disorder and Genius, tr. Kitty Black. London: Hamilton, 1954.

Nausea, tr. Lloyd Alexander. Norfolk: New Directions, 1949.

No Exit and The Flies, tr. Stuart Gilbert, New York: Knopf, 1947.

No Exit and three other plays (*The Flies, Dirty Hands, the Respectful Prostitute*), tr. Lionel Abel. New York: Vintage Books, 1955.

The Respectful Prostitute and Lucifer and the Lord, tr. Kitty Black. Harmondsworth: Penguin Books, 1965.

Three Plays: Crime Passionnel, Men without Shadows, The Respectful Prostitute, tr. Kitty Black. London: Hamilton, 1949.

Three Plays: Dirty Hands, The Respectful Prostitute, The Victors, tr. Lionel Abel. New York: Knopf, 1949.

Saint Genet Actor and Martyr, tr. Bernard Frechtman. New York: Braziller, 1963.

Sartre on Theater. New York: Pantheon, 1976.

Situations, tr. Benita Eisler. New York: Braziller, 1965.

The Wall and other Stories, tr. Lloyd Alexander. New York: New Directions, 1948.

What is Literature?, tr. Bernard Frechtman. New York: Philosophical Library, 1949.

The Words, tr. Bernard Frechtman. New York: Braziller, 1964.

MISCELLANEOUS

Adamov, Arthur. *Théâtre,* I. Paris: Gallimard, 1953.

Alleg, Henri. *La Question.* Paris: Minuit, 1958.

Apollinaire, Guillaume. *Alcools.* Paris: Gallimard, 1920.

Aronson, Ronald. *Jean-Paul Sartre, Philosophy in The World.* London: *NLB,* 1980.

Beauvoir, Simone de. *La Force des Choses.* Paris: Gallimard, 1963.

Beckett, Samuel. *En Attendant Godot.* Paris: Minuit, 1952.
    The Unnamable. New York: Grove, 1958.

Contat, Michel. *Explication des Séquestrés d'Altona.* Paris: Lettres Modernes, 1968.

Contat, Michel, and Michel Rybalka. *Les Ecrits de Sartre.* Paris: Gallimard, 1970.

Descartes, René. *Oeuvres et Lettres.* Paris: Gallimard, 1953.

Duvignaud, Jean. *Le Théâtre et Après.* Tournai: Casterman, 1971.

Genet, Jean. *Les Nègres.* Décines: Barbezat, 1958.
    Oeuvres Complètes, IV. Paris: Gallimard, 1968.

Ionesco, Eugène. *Théâtre,* I. Paris: Gallimard, 1954.

Leblanc, Maurice. *Les Aventures d'Arsène Lupin Gentleman Cambrioleur,* III. Paris: Hachette, 1961.

Lorris, Robert. *Sartre Dramaturge.* Paris: Nizet, 1975.

McCall, Dorothy. *The Theatre of Jean-Paul Sartre.* New York: Columbia University Press, 1969.

Mallarmé, Stéphane. *Oeuvres Complètes.* Paris: Gallimard, 1945.

Sicard, Michel, ed. *Obliques 18-19.* Paris, 1979.

Tardieu, Jean. *Poèmes à Jouer.* Paris: Gallimard, 1960.

Verstraeten, Pierre. *Violence et Ethique, Esquisse d'une Critique de la Morale Dialectique à partir du Théâtre Politique de Sartre.* Paris: Gallimard, 1972.